Carnegie Commission on Higher Education

Sponsored Research Studies

THE AMERICAN COLLEGE AND AMERICAN
CULTURE:
SOCIALIZATION AS A FUNCTION OF HIGHER
EDUCATION
Oscar and Mary F. Handlin

RECENT ALUMNI AND HIGHER EDUCATION:
A SURVEY OF COLLEGE GRADUATES
Joe L. Spaeth and Andrew M. Greeley

CHANGE IN EDUCATIONAL POLICY:
SELF-STUDIES IN SELECTED COLLEGES AND
UNIVERSITIES
Dwight R. Ladd

STATE OFFICIALS AND HIGHER EDUCATION:
A SURVEY OF THE OPINIONS AND
EXPECTATIONS OF POLICY MAKERS IN NINE
STATES
Heinz Eulau and Harold Quinley

ACADEMIC DEGREE STRUCTURES:
INNOVATIVE APPROACHES
PRINCIPLES OF REFORM IN DEGREE
STRUCTURES IN THE UNITED STATES
Stephen H. Spurr

COLLEGES OF THE FORGOTTEN AMERICANS:
A PROFILE OF STATE COLLEGES AND
REGIONAL UNIVERSITIES
E. Alden Dunham

FROM BACKWATER TO MAINSTREAM:
A PROFILE OF CATHOLIC HIGHER
EDUCATION
Andrew M. Greeley

THE ECONOMICS OF THE MAJOR PRIVATE
UNIVERSITIES
William G. Bowen
(Out of print, but available from University Microfilms.)

THE FINANCE OF HIGHER EDUCATION
Howard R. Bowen
(Out of print, but available from University Microfilms.)

ALTERNATIVE METHODS OF FEDERAL
FUND' G FOR HIGHER EDUCATION
Ron Wolk

INVENTORY OF CURRENT RESEARCH ON
HIGHER EDUCATION 1968
Dale M. Heckman and Warren Bryan Martin

The following technical reports are available from the Carnegie Commission on Higher Education, 1947
C er Street, Berkeley, California 94704.

RESOURCE USE IN HIGHER EDUCATION:
TRENDS IN OUTPUT AND INPUTS, 1930–1967
June O'Neill

TRENDS AND PROJECTIONS OF PHYSICIANS
IN THE UNITED STATES 1967–2002
Mark S. Blumberg

MAY 1970:
THE CAMPUS AFTERMATH OF CAMBODIA
AND KENT STATE
Richard E. Peterson and John A. Bilorusky

The following reprints are available from the Carnegie Commission on Higher Education, 1947 Center
Street, Berkeley, California 94704.

ACCELERATED PROGRAMS OF MEDICAL EDUCATION, by Mark S. Blumberg, reprinted from
JOURNAL OF MEDICAL EDUCATION, vol. 46, no. 8, August 1971.

SCIENTIFIC MANPOWER FOR 1970–1985, by Allan M. Cartter, reprinted from SCIENCE, vol.
172, no. 3979, pp. 132–140, April 9, 1971.

A NEW METHOD OF MEASURING STATES' HIGHER EDUCATION BURDEN, by Neil Timm, reprinted
from THE JOURNAL OF HIGHER EDUCATION, vol. 42, no. 1, pp. 27–33, January 1971.

REGENT WATCHING, by Earl F. Cheit, reprinted from AGB REPORTS, vol. 13, no. 6, pp. 4–13,
March 1971.

WHAT HAPPENS TO COLLEGE GENERATIONS POLITICALLY?, by Seymour M. Lipset and Everett
C. Ladd, Jr., reprinted from THE PUBLIC INTEREST, no. 24, Summer 1971.

AMERICAN SOCIAL SCIENTISTS AND THE GROWTH OF CAMPUS POLITICAL ACTIVISM IN THE 1960s, *by Everett C. Ladd, Jr., and Seymour M. Lipset, reprinted from* SOCIAL SCIENCES INFORMATION, *vol. 10, no. 2, April 1971.*

THE POLITICS OF AMERICAN POLITICAL SCIENTISTS, *by Everett C. Ladd, Jr., and Seymour M. Lipset, reprinted from* PS, *vol. 4, no. 2, Spring 1971.*

THE DIVIDED PROFESSORIATE, *by Seymour M. Lipset and Everett C. Ladd, Jr., reprinted from* CHANGE, *vol. 3, no. 3, pp. 54–60, May 1971.*

JEWISH AND GENTILE ACADEMICS IN THE UNITED STATES: ACHIEVEMENTS, CULTURES AND POLITICS, *by Seymour M. Lipset and Everett C. Ladd, Jr., reprinted from* AMERICAN JEWISH YEAR BOOK, *1971.*

THE UNHOLY ALLIANCE AGAINST THE CAMPUS, *by Kenneth Keniston and Michael Lerner, reprinted from* NEW YORK TIMES MAGAZINE, *November 8, 1970 .*

PRECARIOUS PROFESSORS: NEW PATTERNS OF REPRESENTATION, *by Joseph W. Garbarino, reprinted from* INDUSTRIAL RELATIONS, *vol. 10, no. 1, February 1971.*

. . . AND WHAT PROFESSORS THINK: ABOUT STUDENT PROTEST AND MANNERS, MORALS, POLITICS, AND CHAOS ON THE CAMPUS, *by Seymour Martin Lipset and Everett Carll Ladd, Jr., reprinted from* PSYCHOLOGY TODAY, *November 1970.**

DEMAND AND SUPPLY IN U.S. HIGHER EDUCATION: A PROGRESS REPORT, *by Roy Radner and Leonard S. Miller, reprinted from* AMERICAN ECONOMIC REVIEW, *May 1970.**

RESOURCES FOR HIGHER EDUCATION: AN ECONOMIST'S VIEW, *by Theodore W. Schultz, reprinted from* JOURNAL OF POLITICAL ECONOMY, *vol. 76, no. 3, University of Chicago, May/ June 1968.**

INDUSTRIAL RELATIONS AND UNIVERSITY RELATIONS, *by Clark Kerr, reprinted from* PROCEEDINGS OF THE 21ST ANNUAL WINTER MEETING OF THE INDUSTRIAL RELATIONS RESEARCH ASSOCIATION, *pp. 15–25.**

NEW CHALLENGES TO THE COLLEGE AND UNIVERSITY, *by Clark Kerr, reprinted from Kermit Gordon (ed.),* AGENDA FOR THE NATION, *The Brookings Institution, Washington, D.C., 1968. **

PRESIDENTIAL DISCONTENT, *by Clark Kerr, reprinted from David C. Nichols (ed.),* PERSPECTIVES ON CAMPUS TENSIONS: PAPERS PREPARED FOR THE SPECIAL COMMITTEE ON CAMPUS TENSIONS, *American Council on Education, Washington, D.C., September 1970.**

STUDENT PROTEST—AN INSTITUTIONAL AND NATIONAL PROFILE, *by Harold Hodgkinson, reprinted from* THE RECORD, *vol. 71, no. 4, May 1970.**

WHAT'S BUGGING THE STUDENTS?, *by Kenneth Keniston, reprinted from* EDUCATIONAL RECORD, *American Council on Education, Washington, D.C., Spring 1970.**

THE POLITICS OF ACADEMIA, *by Seymour Martin Lipset, reprinted from David C. Nichols (ed.),* PERSPECTIVES ON CAMPUS TENSIONS: PAPERS PREPARED FOR THE SPECIAL COMMITTEE ON CAMPUS TENSIONS, *American Council on Education, Washington, D.C., September 1970.**

The Commission's stock of this reprint has been exhausted.

Professional Education

Professional Education

SOME NEW DIRECTIONS

by Edgar H. Schein

Professor of Organizational Psychology and Management,
Massachusetts Institute of Technology

with the assistance of Diane W. Kommers

Research Assistant, Sloan School of Management,
Massachusetts Institute of Technology

Tenth of a Series of Profiles Sponsored by
The Carnegie Commission on Higher Education

MCGRAW-HILL BOOK COMPANY

New York St. Louis San Francisco Düsseldorf
London Sydney Toronto Mexico Panama
Johannesburg Kuala Lumpur Montreal
New Delhi Rio de Janeiro Singapore

The Carnegie Commission on Higher Education,
1947 Center Street, Berkeley, California 94704,
has sponsored preparation of this profile as a
part of a continuing effort to obtain and present
significant information for public discussion.
The views expressed are those of the authors.

PROFESSIONAL EDUCATION
Some New Directions

Library of Congress Cataloging in Publication Data
Schein, Edgar H.
Professional education: some new directions.

1.   Professional education. I.   Carnegie
Commission on Higher Education. II.   Title.
LC1059.S4   378'.01'3   76-38954
ISBN 0-07-010042-X

123456789MAMM798765432

Contents

Foreword

America's colleges and universities have been preoccupied with problems of growth for several decades. Now, although growth is still a matter of concern, there is increasing preoccupation with change.

That many changes are needed is a matter of widespread agreement. They are required to help higher education adjust to the consequences of its recent rapid expansion and to new expectations of both students and society. There is very little agreement, on the other hand, about what change should be undertaken and how change can be accomplished.

The professions and professional education are particularly interesting subjects for an analysis of the process of change. Professional practice is decreasingly in the single practitioner pattern as more professionals become employees of corporations or work through large organizations. The relationship of professionals to their clients is also changing and the people who pay the fees are less frequently the people who are directly served. The capacity of professionals to learn "everything they need to know" diminishes with the growth of knowledge and development of specialization, and the dependence of the individual practitioner on others in different specialties or even different disciplines is therefore increasing.

The values and needs of professional students are also changing as they seek ways to engage in challenging projects earlier in their careers, as they advocate extending professional services to clients who have been historically underserved, and as they demand more flexible timing for their education and a different pacing and organization of the curriculum.

How should professional schools adapt to these new circumstances and demands? In this report for the Carnegie Commission on Higher Education, Edgar Schein suggests four general directions:

1 More flexibility in the professional school curriculum, in the number of paths available through school, in the number of electives available to students inside and outside the school, in the pacing and sequence of courses, in the required length of time needed to go through school, and in the degree or certification process used by the school

2 More flexibility in the early career paths of professionals, more differentiated rules for licensing to reflect different kinds of professional careers, and more support of role innovation of various kinds by the professions themselves

3 New curricula and new career paths which are inter or transdisciplinary and which may lead eventually to new professions

4 Greater integration of the behavioral and social sciences into the professional school curriculum at three different levels: (1) basic psychology, sociology, anthropology, etc., as a part of the core of professional education; (2) applied behavioral science dealing with the theory and practice of planned change, diagnosis of complex systems, and analysis of client-professional relationships; and (3) applied behavioral science dealing with self-insight, social responsibility, learning how to work in and lead professional teams, and learning how to learn

The Carnegie Commission has already addressed itself to some of these questions in *Less Time, More Options: Education Beyond the High School.* Others will be the subject of reports we now have in preparation.

In this study, Edgar Schein not only elaborates on the innovations he considers necessary for professional education but also describes a model of the processes of change itself. By doing so, he has rendered his study interesting not only to educators in the professional fields, but also to anyone concerned with the problems of effecting change and innovation in higher education.

Clark Kerr
Chairman
The Carnegie Commission
on Higher Education

January 1972

Acknowledgments

This profile was prepared for the Carnegie Commission on Higher Education. The authors acknowledge their indebtedness to Clark Kerr and the Carnegie Commission for their support of the research which led to this report. We also wish to give special thanks to Lotte Bailyn for her conceptual contributions and her critical analysis of parts of this study, and to Fritz Steele for his work on architects and their education.

Professional Education

Part One
The Scope of the Study
and the Diagnosis

As the extent and complexity of the need to provide services to growing numbers of people has become more evident, it has become equally obvious that the problem will not be solved by simply increasing the number of trained professionals or the number of traditional facilities or by increased legislation. Any effort at solution must reconsider the role of the professional, the institutions that train him, and their relationship to the effectiveness of the services offered.

Sheldon K. Schiff, "Training the Professional," 1970

The last several decades have seen a tremendous amount of social and technological change and a tremendous increase in the growth of the professions in response to this change. It is clear that society is becoming more complex, and that this complexity is creating new and pressing social problems. It is equally clear that the growth of basic knowledge and technology has made it possible to attack not only the new problems arising out of this complexity but also old problems that previously remained untouched and sometimes even unrecognized.

The professions have always been the agent by which society dealt with its major problems. It is the professions, therefore, which must continue to change and evolve to deal with new problems and new complexities, using the continually growing knowledge and technological base that is available.

The pressure toward change in the professions can be described from several points of view. As social needs and social institutions have changed, so have the work settings within which professionals operate. No longer does the autonomous professional singly provide his service for a fee; today most professionals are employed in various kinds of organizations and are paid by various combinations of salary and fees. Change in work settings has been accompanied by new concepts of who is the client. Professionals no longer deal exclusively with individual clients; today entire organizations act as purchasers of professional services, and professionals "create" client groups who may not see themselves as clients, such as consumers and ghetto dwellers. Professionals must now relate to multiple client systems and deal with projects in which one part of the client system may conflict with another part of it.

Both the work settings and the type of client have been influenced by the availability of more basic knowledge and more sophisticated technology. Such technology has not only made it possible to work on complex problems which previously seemed insoluble but has also made it necessary for professionals to organize into units large enough to support the capital investment in the technology, e.g., the sophisticated diagnostic equipment of a modern hospital. With the growth of knowledge has come increasing differentiation of the professions into specialties and subspecialties, creating problems of how to integrate the various approaches of the specialist into a coherent professional service. The increase in specialization has created problems of obsolescence, jurisdiction among the professionals, coordination, and too little synergy. Often the specialists work at cross purposes with each other and fail to take advantage of the different points of view that an interdisciplinary approach makes possible.

Changing social values have created new client systems and have led students and young practitioners to call for a rethinking of professional roles. In particular, a higher value is being placed on working for the poor, the ignorant, and the powerless, even if those groups do not see themselves as clients and cannot afford to pay for services. The new values call for the professional to be an advocate, to set about to improve society, not merely to service it, to become more socially conscious, to be more of an initiator than a responder. In these new roles the professional is asked to challenge some of the norms of his own profession and to fight the bureaucratization and standardization that have occurred in many professions.

The kinds of changes we have been describing have affected most of the major professions—medicine, psychiatry, social work, law, architecture, engineering, and teaching. The resulting strains on the professions show up most clearly in professional schools, where some of the faculty and students call for reform and rethinking of professional roles while other faculty and students call for a tightening of professional boundaries and a return to basic concepts and skills. The growing specialization of professional fields has led to some fragmentation of, for example, schools of architecture and schools of engineering, leading to further differentiation of the fields and some recombinations (e.g., of some areas of medicine and some areas of engineering into biomedical engineering). Some segments of the academic community continue to work single-mindedly on basic research while other segments and growing numbers of students are calling for a slowdown of basic research and/or a rethinking of emphasis on new technological advances in terms of their potential social consequences.

In the meantime, the behavioral sciences have made considerable advances in understanding the psychology and sociology of client systems, the processes by which learning and socialization take place, the theory and practice of planned change, the theory and practice of giving and receiving help, group dynamics, and leadership phenomena. All these areas are of increasing relevance to the professions.

The state of ferment in the professions and in the educational establishment makes this a good time to rethink education for the professions. It is increasingly obvious that the professional of the future must have a different set of skills, a different self-image, and a different set of attitudes from the professional of today. How, then, can professional education and early career socialization be redesigned to prepare the professional of tomorrow?

We will attempt to answer this question by first analyzing in somewhat greater detail the traditional concept of the professions and how it has been eroded by rapidly changing social needs, values, and technology (Chapters 1 through 6). In Chapter 7 we will attempt to summarize these trends and to indicate in what ways the professions of tomorrow must be different from the professions of today. Then, in Chapters 8 and 9, we will present a model of the process of planned change. The purpose of this model is to help identify some of the many barriers that will have to be overcome if professional education is to change in the directions recommended and to provide some tools for planning initial steps and points of entry. In Chapters 10 and 11 we focus on educational mechanisms that can and should be used to facilitate the change process toward a new and more relevant kind of professional education. In Chapter 10 we analyze some of the innovations that have been developed and utilized already. In Chapter 11 we present some ideas that are more utopian and will require some new inventions. The different parts of this report have varying degrees of relevance for different kinds of readers. For those readers who wish an analysis of what is happening in the professions, Part 1 (Chapters 1 through 7) would be most relevant. For those readers who are primarily interested in how one might begin to bring about changes in professional education and what new techniques one might try, Part 2 (Chapters 8 through 11) would be more relevant.

A NOTE ON THE METHODOLOGY OF THIS STUDY The basic data for this study are the interview responses of approximately 75 men and women who represent various kinds of professional roles in several major professions — law, medicine, architecture, engineering, management, and university teaching. Primarily we sought out the role innovators (Schein, 1970*b*)— professionals who had been thinking about their own role, its relevance to the needs of today and of the future, and the possibilities of pursuing professional practice in different ways. Many of these people were found on the faculties of professional schools, hence many of our interviewees are professors. Geographically they encompass a wide range; while most of our sample comes from the Northeast, we made a special effort to include people from the West Coast and from overseas. A partial list of the people interviewed is presented in the Appendix. It includes those people who were specifically sought out as part of this study but does not include a great many others whose responses we have been gathering for several years as part of the continuing study of role innovation. The interview responses were supplemented by readings and the results of other studies of professional education.[1]

We faced a basic choice at the outset about depth and breadth of coverage. Some previous studies have surveyed all the professions fairly systematically (Mayhew, 1970*b*; McGlothlin, 1964), while others have taken one profession in depth (Ehrlich & Headrick, 1970; Geddes & Spring, 1967; Perrucci & Gerstl, 1969; Abercrombie, 1967, 1968). We chose a middle ground by focusing primarily on architecture and secondarily on law, medicine, engineering, management, and teaching. This choice was based on an initial assessment that these professions were undergoing parallel and similar kinds of changes. In taking such a comparative perspective, we have had to sacrifice some of the depth of analysis that studies of single professions can provide and instead have attempted a more systematic analysis of the educational problems inherent in the professions generally. Such a focus was supported by our data. Whether we were talking to a lawyer, doctor, or architect, the educational problems of his profession seemed to be the same. We are not claiming, therefore, a full understanding of all the nuances of a given profession; indeed, the very nature of professionalization makes it virtually impossible to understand the subtle nuances of any profession but one's own. We are claiming, however, some insight into the common educational problems that

---

[1] We also checked many of our impressions against the results that are beginning to emerge from a survey of 1,500 MIT alumni. The basic results of this survey will be reported elsewhere, but the data analyses done so far helped to cross-check some of the assertions made by individual interviewees in those professions that were fairly well represented among the alumni.

are inherent in professional education and salient right now in certain key professions, recognizing that any given professional will probably feel that we did not fully understand all the intricacies of his particular set of problems. We can only say, in response, that the data do come from students, practitioners, and teachers in the professions we concentrated on and hence accurately reflect the perspectives of those professionals.

1. What Is a Profession?

Professions *profess.* They profess to know better than others the nature of certain matters, and to know better than their clients what ails them or their affairs.

Everett C. Hughes, "Professions," 1963

The professions are changing, and the education of the future professional is changing. This process can be allowed to happen through a series of evolutionary and revolutionary steps as the needs of society, of students, and of professionals themselves interact. Or the process can be *planned* and *managed* by the professions and the professional schools themselves. It is clearly the spirit of the Carnegie Commission on Higher Education to attempt to understand the changes that are happening and to set about to manage them by specifying some goals to be reached and some strategies and tactics for reaching them.

The major danger in such planning is oversimplification of the problems that hinder constructive change. For example, there is much talk about the need for more interdisciplinary work among professionals and we hear frequent recommendations that professionals should collaborate more. Rarely do we find a clear analysis of why such interdisciplinary, collaborative work is so infrequent or so difficult. There is much talk about the need for more social consciousness in the engineer, the scientist, and the doctor. Rarely do we see an analysis of why those professionals are not more socially conscious in the first place. We hear much talk of educational reform in teacher training, social work training, and psychiatric training. Rarely do we see an analysis of why those reforms have not yet built up much momentum.

The key to understanding the slow rate of change in professional practice and professional education lies in the nature of the professions themselves. The professions are a set of occupations that have developed a very special set of norms deriving from their special role in society. These norms and this special role must be clearly understood if we are to make any sensible and realistic recommendations for planned change.

DEFINING A PROFESSION   Efforts at a clear definition of the concept of professionalism have had a long history. The problem of definition derives from our attempt to give precision to a social or occupational role that varies as a function of the setting within which it is performed, that is itself evolving, and that is perceived differently by different segments of society. Furthermore, the concept of the professional cannot be defined by any single criterion. Different sociologists[1] have given different weights to different criteria, but all have agreed on the necessity to use a multiple criterion definition such as the following:

1   The professional, as distinct from the amateur, is engaged in a *full-time occupation* that comprises his principal source of income.

2   The professional is assumed to have a *strong motivation* or calling as a basis for his choice of a professional career and is assumed to have a stable lifetime commitment to that career.

3   The professional possesses a *specialized body of knowledge and skills* that are acquired during a *prolonged period of education and training.*

4   The professional makes his decisions on behalf of a client in terms of *general principles, theories, or propositions,* which he applies to the particular case under consideration, i.e., by "universalistic" standards, in terms of Parsons' pattern variables (Parsons, 1959).

5   At the same time, the professional is assumed to have a *service orientation,* which means that he uses his expertise on behalf of the particular needs of his client. This service implies diagnostic skill, competent application of general knowledge to the special needs of the client, and an absence of self-interest.

6   The professional's service to the client is assumed to be based on the *objective needs of the client* and independent of the particular sentiments that the professional may have about the client. The professional promises

---

[1] The composite definition or list of criteria presented here is derived from an analysis of the writings of a number of sociologists who have studied the professions intensively during the past several decades, e.g., Goode, 1957; Blau & Scott, 1962; Barber, 1963; Hughes, 1963; Gilb, 1966; Abrahamson, 1967; Parsons, 1968; Gross, 1969; Moore, 1970; Wilensky, 1964.

a "detached" diagnosis. The client is expected to be fully frank in revealing potentially unlikeable things about himself; the professional as his part of the contract is expected to withhold moral judgment, no matter how he may feel personally about the client's revelation. Thus, the professional relationship rests on a kind of *mutual trust between the professional and client.*

7   The professional is assumed to know better what is good for the client than the client himself. In other words, the professional demands *autonomy of judgment of his own performance.* Even if the client is not satisfied, the professional will, in principle, permit only his colleagues to judge his performance. Because of this demand for professional autonomy, the client is in a potentially vulnerable position. How does he know whether he has been cheated or harmed? The profession deals with this potential vulnerability by developing strong ethical and professional standards for its members. Such standards may be expressed as codes of conduct and are usually enforced by colleagues through professional associations or through licensing examinations designed and administered by fellow professionals.

8   Professionals form *professional associations which define criteria of admission, educational standards, licensing or other formal entry examinations, career lines within the profession, and areas of jurisdiction* for the profession. Ultimately, the professional association's function is to protect the autonomy of the profession; it develops reasonably strong forms of self-government by setting rules or standards for the profession.

9   Professionals have great power and status in the area of their expertise, but their *knowledge is assumed to be specific.* A professional does not have a license to be a "wise man" outside the area defined by his training.

10   Professionals make their service available but ordinarily are *not allowed to advertise or to seek out clients.* Clients are expected to initiate the contact and then accept the advice and service recommended, without appeal to outside authority.

As can be seen, these various criteria fit best the traditional, ancient, or "learned" professions of medicine, law, and divinity. They fit in varying degrees professions like architecture, social work, engineering, teaching, and management. Moore (1970) has proposed that the above criteria (particularly numbers 1, 2, 8, 3, 5, and 7, in that order) be arranged as a kind of *scale* of professionalization, thus permitting one to judge any given occupational group in terms of its "degree of professionalization."

The ultimate criterion of professionalization according to most sociologists is the achievement of "autonomy," which implies (1) knowing better what is good for the client than anyone else because of extended technical education or training, (2) subjecting one's decisions only to the review of colleagues, and (3) setting all one's standards pertaining to jurisdiction of the profession and entry into it through peer-group associations. These characteristics give rise to professional "communities," implying a common sense of identity, self-regulation, lifetime membership, shared values, a common language, clear social boundaries, and strong socialization of new members (Goode, 1957).

Let us look at several examples of how these criteria apply to different professions. Some fields of *medicine* fit *every* criterion mentioned. Typically, a doctor is fully committed to a lifetime career in medicine. He has a body of specialized knowledge acquired over a prolonged period of education, internship, and residency, and he applies his knowledge in an objective manner to the needs of each patient, even if the patient is not able to pay full fees. He takes a detached, neutral attitude toward the patient, is highly autonomous, is willing to subject his judgments *only* to the review of fellow doctors, and has a strong ethical code inculcated throughout school and early career training. He belongs to a professional association that has been very influential in setting the standards for licensing at a sufficiently high level to protect the profession from encroachment by laymen or competitors such as osteopaths or chiropractors. He recognizes that his expertise is limited to the delivery of medical care and believes that the patient should initiate the contact with the doctor unless special circumstances are involved such as an emergency, an accident, an epidemic, or admission into an organization that requires a medical examination.

Management, in contrast, fits very few of the criteria. Management may or may not be a full-time career, may or may not have been entered with a strong sense of calling, and often does *not* involve a specialized body of knowledge and a long period of formal training.[2] Managers have no clear definition of the client on whose behalf they are to work—whether the client is society, the consumer, the stockholders, the employing organization, the manager's

---

[2] There is a trend toward speaking of "professional" managers. This derives from the fact that many managers have at least two years of graduate training at a business or management school and implies that they have access to a particular body of expert knowledge that can be used on behalf of any of a number of different organizations.

immediate superior, his peers, his subordinates, or ultimately the "profession" of management itself (Schein, 1966). The manager does not have a service orientation unless one defines the employing organization as the client. He is presumed to be guided primarily by self-interest except at higher levels of management, but he is also expected to deliver a detached, objective service to the company. (If the manager is morally unable to accept the organization's goals, he is expected to terminate employment.) The manager is clearly not autonomous but, rather, subjected to constant review by *superior* authority. Managers have not developed a code of ethics or standards (partly because of the ambiguity of who is the client), do not limit their range of expertise, and do not avoid self-advertisement. By these criteria, then, management is barely beginning to professionalize itself.

Between management and medicine is a range of professions like engineering and teaching that are more professionalized than management in the sense that they clearly involve a body of expert knowledge and skills learned over a period of time, imply a set of ethics or standards of professional practice, and *attempt* to maintain their professional autonomy. However, the fact that most engineers and teachers work for large organizations rather than small professional offices makes it unclear precisely who their client is, erodes their autonomy, and weakens colleague authority in favor of line authority within the employing organization. In the case of engineering there is also less sense of calling and more acknowledgement that engineering as a career may merely be a stepping stone toward better paid and higher status managerial jobs.[3]

Because of the lack of clear norms of entry into the profession, the path into engineering may be highly variable and may involve bypassing advanced education and higher degrees. Licensing or registering of engineers is generally not required by large industrial employers (who probably feel that they can control performance directly through administrative authority), but it is required where engineers set up consulting practices which deal with clients who

---

[3] In a recent survey of MIT graduates of 1951, 1955, and 1959, we found evidence that remaining in a technical field as an engineer or scientist was not rewarded by salary or status. Even if the engineers had Ph.D.'s they were paid less than technical managers with a bachelor's degree. Subjective ratings of career success and job satisfaction were also lower in the group that stayed in purely technical jobs (Bailyn, Schein, & Siler, 1971).

are more vulnerable to poor performance by the engineers.[4] Thus, the degree to which engineering and teaching are professionalized depends upon the setting in which they are practiced, the manner in which practitioner performance is controlled, and the manner in which they were entered (Perrucci & Gerstl, 1969).

The *academic profession,* i.e., the university professor, is closer to the medical model than to the engineering or the managerial model. It involves a full-time occupation, a sense of calling, a long period of education, specialized knowledge, a service orientation toward students, strong *informal* criteria for "licensing" via the granting of tenure by colleagues, assumed ethical standards, autonomy, review only by colleagues, specific expertise rather than general wisdom, and lack of self-advertisement. The profession is ambiguous, however, in that it involves several roles within a role and a nebulous client concept.

In his role as *teacher,* the professor has a mission (teaching), but he has neither professional training as a teacher nor a well-defined client. In one sense the student is his client, but he often deals with students as a general client category, not as individuals with particular problems. Yet much of what the teacher decides to do vis-à-vis his students is predicated upon the assumption that it is his job to fulfill society's needs for a responsible and well-educated citizen; hence, in another sense, society is the real client. Many teachers try to excite students about their particular discipline and select material on the basis of what they feel the student should know if he is to pursue that discipline; in this case, teachers are trying to meet the needs of the discipline or field as the real client. The field of teaching does not have clear norms as to which of these clients is to be served.

---

[4] The engineer's sense of professional identity is further undermined by the wide variety of specialties that exists in engineering, making it difficult to identify common concerns and common bases of knowledge. Furthermore, the engineer's activities are so varied from basic design to development to supervision of production that it is difficult to specify which of those activities should be the subject of ethical codes. Even if such codes could be written, there would be no practical way to enforce them.

". . . it has been found that engineering registration boards are sometimes lax in their administration of the laws, that engineering societies are not uniformly in favor of registration; that engineers, both registered and unregistered, do not feel very strongly in favor of registration; that only about one fourth of all engineers are registered; that the proportion registered has remained constant from 1940 to 1965; and that registration is most likely among engineers legally required to register" (Rothstein, 1969, p. 85).

In his role as *scholar/researcher,* the professor has had long professional training which has created internalized standards and a powerful sense of autonomy; but here again, who is the client to whom the service is delivered? Is the scientist working in a university functionally in the same profession as the scientist working in industry? Or does the university scientist align himself more with professional colleagues in other universities while the industrial scientist aligns himself with his employing organization?

In many fields such as engineering, medicine, and law, the professor may also function as a *consultant* to government, industry, or other organizations. In this role, the professor operates much like the M.D. except that once again he is not trained specifically in the practice of delivering the consulting service. Furthermore, if the client is an industrial concern or a government unit, the meaning of "providing a service to a client" has a different implication because the client system is often seeking the service in connection with an economic or policy goal that may or may not be in the best interest of some other segments of society.[5]

As our final example, let us examine *architecture* because it is in greater flux in modern society. The architect in private practice building homes for individual homeowners fits most of the criteria of the professional with the following exceptions: (1) he may have acquired his training informally through a long period of apprenticeship rather than a formal professional education leading to a specific academic degree; and (2) his client is clearly the individual who is paying for his services, but, because publicly visible buildings are involved, the architect may be constrained by zoning ordinances, building codes, the need to integrate the new building aesthetically with the surrounding environment, and his own assumptions about what is functional and aesthetic. The paying client's needs are, in other words, partially modified by the needs of the architect himself and the needs of the surrounding community.

As the work settings of professionals change, these problems

[5] Consider, for example, the radical student's efforts to minimize the involvement of the university in defense contracts. From the radical's point of view the professor is working directly for certain clients who, the radical feels, should not be entitled to the services of the professional. From the professor's point of view he is, of course, not working for the sponsoring agency as a direct client, but even if he were, the traditional concept of professional practice would make the idea of *selective* help to client systems based on their politics, etc., an entirely alien concept.

become more complex. For example, when the architect works for a real estate developer, a city school committee, or an urban re-development authority, it is unclear who the "real" client is whose needs should be given top priority. Consequently, as in the case of management, it is difficult to specify ethical standards or criteria by which professional decisions are to be made. If the architect is working for a private organization such as a large planning firm, it becomes even more difficult to specify who is the client, whether or not professionally set standards of practice apply, whether or not the architect has any professional autonomy, and whether or not he will be responsive to a professional association or even belong to one. As in the case of engineering, it has even been difficult to *form* associations which would set standards and force adherence to them through enforced registration because of the employer's willingness to hire unregistered engineers (Gross, 1969).

In summary, it is not as easy to define what constitutes a profession as one might at first assume. The ideal model to which most professions aspire can be described, but it rarely applies in practice and is itself shifting. If we are to understand these trends, we must next analyze more closely the work settings of professionals and the shifting nature of the client or client systems.

2. The Changing Work Setting of Professionals

In the United States, most professions are and always have been practiced in an organization by salaried employees.

> Edward Gross, "Change in Technological and Scientific Developments and Its Impact upon the Social Structure," 1969, p. 35

Many of the analyses of the professions perpetuate the assumption that a professional is an autonomous practitioner dealing with a single fee-paying client who has come to the professional for some form of help. The professional is assumed to be working in an office by himself or to be loosely associated with a few colleagues in similar or related professions. Engineering, which, as we have noted, usually involves working for a large organization, tends to be viewed as an exception or as less professional by virtue of the employee status of the individual engineer. Only recently have we begun to acknowledge that the employment settings of most professionals have shifted dramatically away from the single-practitioner model toward corporate employment.

To get a feel for the consequences of this shift, let us first examine the variety of employment settings in which professionals find themselves.

1 *Full-time self-employed*—e.g., the general practitioner, small-town lawyer, or individual consulting architect

2 *Part-time self-employed; part-time employee of service organization* (i.e., organization that is devoted to delivery of the professional service)—e.g., the internist with a private practice as well as membership on the staff of the local hospital, the consulting architect who teaches part-time in the local university

3   *Partner in a group practice*—e.g., the small architectural or law firm, or a medical group practice involving several M.D.'s in the same speciality or in complementary specialties

4   *Full-time employee of a service organization devoted to the delivery of the professional service*—e.g., a full-time member of a teaching hospital; an employee—*not* partner—of a large, well-differentiated law, architectural, or planning firm; a professor in a college or university

5   *Employee of an organization not primarily devoted to the delivery of the professional service*—e.g., the doctor, lawyer, architect, or engineer working for a business firm or government department[1]

6   *Employee of a professional association*—e.g., president of the American Medical Association (AMA), executive secretary of the American Psychological Association, full-time examiner on a licensing board

The distinctions in work settings are important because they strongly influence the professional's self-image, his definition of the client, and his conception of the proper way to relate to the client. The self-employed professional deals directly with the client who comes to him voluntarily on a one-to-one basis. If the professional is a member of a group practice, he continues to be primarily oriented to the interests of the individual client, but there is a potential conflict of interests between what is best for the client and what is best for the survival, economic health, and growth of the group practice. If, for example, referral to another specialist is involved, the individual practitioner must balance the needs of the client for the best possible professional service with the needs of his own group for additional business. Can he remain objective in this context?[2] In other words, the group practice itself becomes in part a client system to which the professional must respond.

If the professional is an employee of a hospital, his ability to deliver a fully autonomous service will depend very much upon the norms of the particular organization which employs him. He may be able to promise the client a much better total service because he

---

[1] There are a number of different work settings *within* such organizations that must themselves be distinguished. We will return to this point later.

[2] Of course, the same problem arises with the individual practitioner—does he refer patients to the best possible specialist or to his friends who may need some business? In group practice this conflict is more apparent, however, because it involves the financial self-interest of the practitioner.

will presumably be more current on latest advances in the field and have access to better equipment by virtue of being part of a group; on the other hand, the client will probably be committed to accepting related services about which he has no choice,[3] and he may even have to accept as his prime contact any of a number of practitioners simply on the basis of who is available. In this case the needs of the organization clearly play some role in how the professional dispenses his services, but the organization as a whole is assumed to work on behalf of the client. To protect himself the client must then evaluate not only his own doctor but the hospital with which the doctor is affiliated. Often he will choose the individual doctor *because* of his affiliation with a high-reputation hospital.

If the professional works for a corporation or government office, his *primary* client is his employer. In this case he sells his service to the employer on the *assumption* that the products or services produced by the employer are of ultimate benefit to the consumer or the public at large. There are two kinds of internal professional roles. The doctor may be hired to provide his services in the traditional one-to-one fashion to the other *employees* of the organization; the military chaplain is employed to serve the individual members of a particular military unit. In this case, the issue is whether or not the service *can* be dispensed objectively or whether it is inevitably biased by the needs of the employing organization. Doctors who find a heart condition in a senior executive may have to decide whether to let anyone other than the patient know about his condition. If the executive is in line for a more responsible job in which his ill health could jeopardize the well-being of the company, is the doctor obligated to report the condition to top management? Chaplains and psychiatrists in the military service have sometimes been accused of "adjusting" the attitudes of soldiers toward their fighting role rather than helping the individual soldier to achieve a personal sense of integration even if this means a pacifist set of attitudes. Social workers have faced the dilemma of whether to stimulate self-actualization or to help the client adjust to his condi-

---

[3] Many architectural firms develop a certain design style or preferences for certain materials which give the firm its professional identity. The individual architect can exercise autonomy of design only within the limits set by the firm's policies, though these limits may not be made public or presented to the client as an initial set of constraints.

tion, no matter how marginal it might be. In all these cases, there is potential conflict between the needs of the individual client and the needs of the organization, but the basic service is still performed for a set of *individual* clients.

The second case of professionals working for government or industry involves a further shift of role. The doctor who works for the pharmaceutical company in the development and marketing of a product, the researcher in an industrial or government laboratory, the minister who writes literature for the Office of the Chaplain in Washington, and the engineer who designs and helps build consumer products all fit this second employee category. The immediate client is the employing organization and the ultimate client is the consumer of the product or service; but while the professional is responsible to the immediate client, he has no direct contact at all with the ultimate client.[4]

In these work settings the professional, especially the engineer or scientist, is typically caught in a conflict between considerations of *elegance of solution* (his own professional need), *quality of the product* (the needs of the ultimate consumer), and considerations of *cost and speed of getting into production* (the needs of his employer). The potential conflict between these considerations has been clearly articulated and exemplified by Ralph Nader's investigations of scientists in private or government laboratories who test products for ultimate commercial use. Nader cites examples of organizational pressures on individual scientists to suppress or distort their findings, voluntary suppression or distortion by scientists because they fear loss of job, and actual falsification or suppression of information at higher levels without the knowledge of the scientists concerned (Nader, 1967; Boffey, 1970).

The important point to recognize is that when the professional works for an organization, he loses not only direct client contact but also control over his own professional output. Once the engineer, scientist, or architect has produced a solution to a problem, his employer can do what he wishes with that solution. Consequently, even if the professional works in a completely responsible way

[4] An interesting case is that of Albert Speer, Hitler's architect. In his memoirs Speer outlines in poignant detail some of his role conflict, especially toward the end of the war when Hitler wanted European cities destroyed, while Speer, thinking in broader "client" terms, decided to save them even at the risk of directly disobeying Hitler (Speer, 1970).

(from the ultimate client's point of view), he cannot control modifications or alternative uses to which his work may be put.[5]

The final work setting to be discussed is that of the professional association itself. More and more professionals take part- or full-time positions within the local or national office of their professional association as executive secretaries, researchers, program managers, or committee chairmen (Gilb, 1966). In such a capacity the professional may have no client contact at all, or, alternatively, he may define the entire profession as his client.

The initial purpose of a professional association is usually to protect and enhance the profession through (1) defining its boundaries and setting entrance criteria, (2) lobbying with local government for varying degrees of autonomy or self-government by setting up and legalizing licensing procedures, and (3) conducting essentially public relations activities on behalf of the profession (Gilb, 1966). However, as these associations mature, they often prescribe norms which are *presumed* to be good for the professional and client alike yet which may be in the interests of neither. For example, it is not clear whether some of the political stands of the AMA in regard to Medicare and socialized medicine have been of benefit either to the public or to the profession of medicine (Gilb, 1966; Crichton, 1970). Similarly, the very tight admissions requirements of some of the psychoanalytic institutes have been deplored both by potential patients in need of help and young analysts seeking to provide the help.

The professional association tends to take a conservative stand with respect to the profession because that is its primary function and because it tends to attract as employees senior members of the profession who are less in touch with the current requirements for

[5] In a speech, Ralph Nader has called for "internal whistle blowing" by employed scientists and engineers (Boffey, 1971). Nader feels that professional standards should make the individual scientist or engineer expose his own employer if he is aware of any neglect of ultimate consumer interests, though he acknowledges the difficulty of such whistle blowing in the absence, inside organizations, of the normal protections of due process which the citizen has vis-à-vis civil government (Evan, 1962). Only if professional associations or new kinds of legal protection for employees were to make the situation safe for the internal professional could one expect such behavior to occur. Even then, the professional might not be able to overcome the organizational socialization to which he has been subjected for the better part of his career. One cannot assume that purely professional loyalty will remain high after many years of employment in a large organization.

the delivery of professional services. In addition, as the professional acquires *managerial* responsibility, he tends to lose identification with the profession as a whole and to increase in identification with the particular organization which employs him.

It is quite clear that as the work setting of professionals shifts toward employment in large organizations, professional autonomy is eroded and new concepts of responsibility to clients must be developed. This trend may or may not be desirable from the point of view of either the professional or the client, yet because of technological, economic, and social forces, the trend exists. As Gilb (1966, p. 98) puts it:

Technological advances, the bulk of new knowledge, the availability of capital, socioeconomic changes that have made large-scale undertakings more feasible as well as necessary—these and other factors have altered the old ways of dispensing services. Whatever the causes, all of the contemporary pressures for change seemed to point in the same direction: away from the guild model of an independent practitioner who directly serves those who consume his services, and who is regulated primarily by his peers, and toward the collectivization of professional work. To serve greatly increased demands, to provide continuity of service over longer spans of time, to permit coordination of workers, to allow work on projects of larger size, to make possible greater use of expensive equipment, to centralize and perhaps automate administration of clerical work, to correlate professional work with other kinds of service—for all of these purposes it has become more feasible to administer prepayment for services on a large scale through a third party, to bring larger numbers of professional workers into a going organization as salaried adjuncts.

In summary, the basic definition of a professional is more than a matter of applying a number of complex criteria since the many settings within which professionals do their work are changing some of the very criteria by which their role was defined in the first place. To put this matter another way, as society is becoming more differentiated and complex, the work roles of professionals are becoming more varied and complex. This complexity generates forces toward differentiation of the professions into many more specialties, creates jurisdictional problems among professions and among specialties within professions, forces new definitions of the proper role of the professional and his proper responsibility to clients, and creates the need for more integrators to coordinate the efforts of different specialists.

3. New Clients, New Client Needs

As we have pointed out, the role of the professional has been changing because of a correlated and interdependent set of changes in society. Problems which previously were not even acknowledged as legitimately in the domain of a given profession are now being recognized and defined as legitimate and important areas of concern (e.g., the treatment of illegitimate pregnancy through abortion, the efforts to correct social decay in urban ghettos, etc.). More complex technology and changing social values have made it possible and desirable to tackle complex social problems. But as more complex problems are tackled, it becomes more difficult for the professions to retain a clear picture of precisely who their clients are. Since the essence of professionalism is the delivery of a service in response to client need, it becomes critical, if the professional is to retain his sense of professional identity, to identify clearly on whose behalf services are being rendered. Furthermore, standards and ethics surrounding professional practice usually develop in direct proportion to the clarity and vulnerability of the client. If new clients are emerging and if clients develop new needs, we must examine the impact of those changes on professional standards and ethics.

In the previous chapter we pointed out that traditional assumptions about the professions always involved the individual fee-paying client seeking medical, legal, architectural, or other services. We pointed out that professions are increasingly doing their work in organizational settings as salaried employees, and we identified some of the conflicts which professionals face in deciding whether their responsibility is to their employer or to the client seeking help. It is the purpose of this chapter to examine in greater detail the issues surrounding the client and to assess their impact on the professions.

We can identify several important shifts in the definition of the term *client:*

1 The client is frequently an *organization* or *larger social system,* such as a city, that is purchasing a service on behalf of a category of people, such as citizens of a given community, renters of apartments in a large housing development, or consumers of a manufactured product.

2 The client is frequently an ambiguous *series of individuals and/or organizations* that lies along a scale running from "immediate contact client" to "ultimate client" or ultimate consumer of a given service, such as in the above example in which a housing authority is the immediate client, the city government and community are intermediate clients, and occupants are ultimate clients. Furthermore, different clients along this scale can be and often are in conflict with each other, creating a real dilemma for the professional as to whose interests he must ultimately be concerned about.

3 The client, either individual or organizational, is frequently less dependent and/or vulnerable than he once was with respect to some professions, but is more dependent and/or vulnerable with respect to others.

ORGANIZA-
TION AS
CLIENT
The fully employed, salaried professional in private industry or in government has as his client his employing organization. In every sense of the concept, his service is delivered to the employing organization, and the professional has little say over the ultimate disposition of this service. The management of the organization sets the policy and the only real choice open to the professional is whether or not to remain with the organization. This concept clearly applies to the engineer in private industry, the architect working for urban redevelopment agencies, the chemist or doctor working in the industrial or government research laboratory, and the teacher in a tightly controlled school.

A somewhat less obvious but equally common case involves the purchase of professional services on a fee or contract basis by an organization. In this case the professional retains much more autonomy than he would as a salaried employee, but his client is still an organization as a whole and his product may be disposed of in ways that the professional may not foresee and cannot control. For example, a planning firm, real estate developer, or redevelopment authority may hire architects or planners to produce designs that may be *used* by them according to entirely different assumptions than those held by the architect.

The above problem is particularly relevant to those professions that make available a service in the form of a product, design, or set of ideas that can be used after the client-professional contact is officially terminated. It thus applies especially to engineering, architecture, research and scholarship, professional consulting in the area of management, personnel and organization development, and teaching. It applies less to medicine and law unless we are considering medical or legal procedures that are broadly applicable, such as a case which sets a wide precedent or a surgical technique such as organ transplant which, once invented, becomes available to everyone. Professionals push ahead in all these areas with only a vague notion of how their service will in fact influence or be used by the members of the organization for whom the service is performed.

This issue underlies the frequently voiced concern about utilization of scientific and technological knowledge. Scientists and engineers may be initially stimulated to work in certain areas because of research contracts that reflect the foundation's or government agency's desire to add to our store of basic knowledge and technology, viewing *society* as the client or ultimate beneficiary. But once the knowledge is available, there is no guarantee that it will be used only as originally intended. Hence there is lively debate concerning the social responsibility of scientists and engineers.

In principle this kind of problem has existed just as much with the individual client. Individuals hire lawyers to evade taxes, doctors to do plastic surgery to avoid capture by the police, and engineers to build better weapons for illegal activities. However, it is much easier for the professional to evaluate the motives and intentions of the individual client than of the organizational client. Much of the ethical training of the professional is built on the individual-client model, and the professional is trained to diagnose the intentions of individual clients. As organizations increasingly play the client role, professional training and education will increasingly have to teach practitioners how to assess and evaluate *organizational* intentions.

IMMEDIATE, INTERMEDIATE, AND ULTIMATE CLIENTS Closely correlated with the growth of organizations as clients is the phenomenon of professional services that are initially commissioned by one client system (the immediate or contact client) and are evaluated by an intermediate client system even though they are carried out in behalf of some ultimate user of the products of the service (ultimate client). A simple example is the commissioning of a technical team by the research and development department of a company (the immediate client) to design a new product or service. The solution is evaluated and further developed by various managers within the company, representing marketing, sales, production, and financial interests, and by development engineers (intermediate client). The consumer for whom the product or service is being developed, however, is the ultimate client for whose benefit the professional service was presumably commissioned. A more complex example is the hiring of an architect by a real estate firm to build low-cost housing with the aid of federal funds administered through a local housing authority. The real estate firm is the immediate client; the housing authority is the intermediate client; and the low-income tenant is the ultimate client. This example can be further complicated by considering as intermediate clients the local planning authority which attempts to integrate the housing development aesthetically into some larger plan for the city and the local city government which considers the tax-base implications of the development. An additional ultimate client is the public at large, which wants a housing development that will not only be aesthetically pleasing but will reduce some of the social ills of the ghetto.

This complexity of multiple client systems leads to several issues or questions for the professional: (1) Which one or more of the clients does the professional define as his *real* client? (2) If the needs of immediate, intermediate, and ultimate clients are in conflict with each other, how does the professional reconcile these conflicts? (3) If the ultimate client is not the one who pays the professional fees, can his interests be properly represented (i.e., can he be the real client, or is he usually ranked lower on the list of client systems)? (4) If professional standards or ethics are to be applied to client-professional relationships, how are these to be applied if they differ for different client systems? (5) Can a professional work for a multiple-client system?

The needs of the ultimate client, the consumer or user, usually conflict in some way with those of the immediate or intermediate clients, though their stated goals may be the same. The consumer wants high quality, low price, safe and relevant products; the company wants products that will sell in large volume, with a good price-cost ratio, at an acceptable level of quality. The individual scientist, engineer, or designer is caught in the middle—the professional standards or ethics that apply to the ultimate client are usually out of line with the requirements of his immediate employer.

To give another example, the low-income tenant wants inexpensive, flexible housing that will permit the expression of his cultural norms and values; the real estate developer wants housing that will not be too expensive to construct and will, therefore, use standard modules and cheap materials—he will be guided by efficiency, not by relevance to the cultural values of the tenants; the housing authority wants housing that will fit into its overall master plan of urban development and its set of assumptions about the needs of the ghetto dweller, assumptions that may or may not reflect actual needs. The architect will also be highly responsive to his own assumptions and to the style of his firm in order to create a solution which will do him and his firm credit and which will be aesthetically pleasing to various observers. Given these forces, it is unlikely that the ghetto dweller's needs and culture will be high on the list of client concerns to be taken into account.

In recent decades, however, there has been a shift in social values toward more consideration of the ultimate client. Advocacy law, or public-interest law as practiced by Ralph Nader and John Banzhaf and advocacy architecture as practiced by Robert Goodman and Chester Sprague start with the clear assumption that the consumer or user has certain rights to be protected from unsafe products, unfair advertising, misleading packaging, and excessive paternalism.[1] There is a correlated change in attitudes toward the poor person in our society. As poverty is increasingly perceived to be society's responsibility, the poor person is perceived as having rights to a decent environment and legal protection rather than as deserving punishment for his poverty. If society is perceived as responsible, then the professions become responsible for providing a full range of services to the poor and the powerless—services paid for by foundations or by national or local government.[2]

---

[1] See Nader, 1969; Page, 1970; Goodman, 1969; Sprague, 1970.

[2] In one of Ralph Nader's television reports dealing with a town completely dominated by a benevolent, paternalistic company, he raises the interesting issue of whether the citizens of that town should be awakened to their lack of freedom even if they don't feel the constraints. Nader's investigators found that all public buildings were owned by the company, that there were few public officials and those few were occupying company-owned offices, that there were no other jobs available, and that subtle pressures were put on any employee who disagreed with company policy. Yet the citizens were better off than they would have been without the company there and most of them felt very good about the services provided by the company. Nader argued that the citizens of this town were not getting any basic education in citizenship and that the company had in fact an obligation to stimulate self-government, unionism, and other self-help mechanisms in order to emancipate the citizens from their dependence.

In architecture this historical development has been described by several professors of architecture in the following way:[3]

Architecture historically was used for the creation of special environments for a limited number of people who could afford such environments. The heroic model of the architect was usually the older man who was a brilliant designer/thinker, who could put his ideas into words, and gather around him strong but subservient colleagues and subordinates. The designer was the unquestioned leader of the design team, even if it involved other specialties or professions. His work was usually limited to the middle- and upper-class client or the large business concern that could afford expensive designs. This model worked well because the architect usually had empathy for those who were at his own or higher socioeconomic levels. He knew their style of life from his own experience and could therefore design with conviction. The architect saw his goal, from a narcissistic and exhibitionistic viewpoint, as an opportunity to enlarge himself through his creations.

Housing for the poor was, of course, also designed by architects but rarely by prominent ones, and rarely with a philosophy of creating something beautiful that would make the architect proud. Instead, design was dominated by a kind of punishment philosophy—if you are poor, you don't deserve anything better than the marginal housing you are given. If low-income housing were too attractive, it might undermine the dweller's desire to work himself up the socioeconomic ladder and lead to complacency among the poor. Supporting this philosophy was the harsh reality of how low-income housing was financed. It was usually commissioned and paid for by housing authorities dominated by local politicians whose success depended in part upon conserving the taxpayers' money. If low-income housing were too attractive, it was assumed that the taxpayer would become critical of the housing authority for spending too much money on such housing.

Changes in this philosophy can be traced to the Kennedy era in which liberal politicians articulated a new philosophy that life should be pleasant even for the poor, and that they should have some voice in determining the kind of environment in which they would live. Here, as in law, we have the new idea that a client can be "created" by being involved, even though that "client" may initially be unaware of his own need and may be unable to pay professional fees. Correlated with this shifting client concept has been a shift away from the heroic image of the lone designer surrounded by armies of draftsmen toward an image of the architect as a functioning member of a design team in which other professions and specialties play a role as important as the design role. This shift has been stimulated by the

[3] The above is paraphrased from several interviews of professors of architecture conducted at the University of California and MIT.

growing complexity of the planning and design task and the increasing interdependence among various experts who are needed to make today's complex and large-scale projects work. Not only is there less of an ethos to glorify the lone central hero, à la *The Fountainhead,* but there is a growing sense of egalitarianism among the various professionals within the architectural office.

As the client concept shifts to more concern for the ultimate client, a new dilemma faces the architect. Whereas he had empathy for clients at his own or higher socioeconomic levels, he often lacks empathy for the low-income groups he is trying to serve today. He does not have feeling for the environment and therefore lacks design confidence. Consequently he must, if he is to improve the environment of the poor, learn more about the sociology of the poor and how to work collaboratively with them. *The involvement of the client in the redesign of his own environment is therefore not just a philosophical principle but a practical necessity,* and the education of the professional must change to train him for such collaborative roles. [4]

A correlated dilemma is that working for clients who cannot pay high fees necessitates a different structure for financing the professional services through public, private, or foundation funds. Obtaining government funds requires collaboration with various intermediate clients who often place specific constraints on how funds are used and who often require much more clearly articulated solutions to design questions than the individual client would demand. Whereas the architect could simply reassure his individual client that he would love his house once it was built, working on large-scale publicly financed projects requires detailed documentation and solutions that can stand up to the criticism of politicians, other architects, and government officials. The architect must, therefore, not only have the design skills and the collaborative ability to work with his clients and fellow team members but he must also be able to negotiate with the complex organizational system of housing authorities, government departments, and local community organizations.

---

[4] An interesting example of such collaboration in medicine occurs in plastic surgery when both patient and doctor have a voice in the outcome. More recently we have heard that in cases of breast cancer in which breast removal is not certain to produce a cure, surgeons are genuinely involving patients in decisions traditionally defined as purely medical decisions.

A vivid example comes from one professor of architecture who is helping various Indian tribes to become involved in the design of their schools, homes, and other buildings commissioned for them by the Bureau of Indian Affairs. This architect must first establish the trust of the Indians to obtain their active involvement; he must work collaboratively with the Association of American Indian Affairs to obtain necessary funds, and he must work with educators, economists, and lawyers who are also involved with the Indian tribes in helping to shape the program into a total community development effort. As this man puts it, his biggest problem is not with the Indians or the bureaucrats but with the other professionals, especially the educators who are used to telling the client exactly what to do. This architect has come to accept the principle of the community's control over its own affairs but finds that other professionals are less ready to accept this principle.

The lone architect or the partner in a small architectural firm is in a highly vulnerable position if he depends on *publicly* financed projects because of the unreliability of obtaining such funds over a period of years. Consequently, some architects find themselves in a real conflict as to whether they should continue to serve the low-income ultimate client or whether they should retreat to more traditional concepts of practice, building middle- and upper-level private and commercial buildings paid for by individuals or business concerns. It is pressures like these which probably cause many more professionals to work as salaried employees of larger, more stable organizations, even though in architecture the salaried practitioner is definitely considered of lower status than the independent designer with his own office.

A different solution followed by some professionals is to define the client-professional relationship as an inherently collaborative one and to begin to invent systems and procedures that can be generally applied across a wide variety of client systems to help clients become involved in the design of their own environments or other services. For example, such procedures might involve modular construction methods that permit a client to select house components much as he might select furniture and to pay according to the combination of components which he selects. Some doctors with a similar set of notions have sought to invent health care *systems* that rely heavily on paraprofessionals or computer-aided diagnostic devices; thus the doctor himself need not treat each patient.

The professional reorientation described above often involves simultaneously more concern for the user, especially the "disenfranchised user," and concern for the community in which he lives, on the assumption that the user's welfare is intimately related to the welfare of his community. Thus, the architect working with the Indians defines his project as "community development." In a similar vein, some social work agencies are explicitly redefining their client as the entire *community* rather than as the *individual family*, again on the assumption that so many of the difficulties of the individual family are community-related that one must start with the community itself as the target of services. For example, the New York Community Service Agency, one of the city's oldest private social agencies, recently announced that it would terminate all family casework and individual counseling (*The New York Times*, January 29, 1971). Instead, the agency is explicitly defining the community as its client and is setting out to invent those kinds of services that will be of most use to the community as a whole (e.g., day-care centers, "learning to read" programs for children, training courses in bookkeeping or home economics, and advocacy with local and national government on behalf of community groups).

In a similar vein, some of the health care centers now being developed in the inner city attempt to deliver total health care services to *all* members of a given part of the city through professional teams (Fry & Lech, 1971). The Harvard Medical School developed a health insurance plan, the Harvard Community Health Program, which is a group-practice plan with a unique emphasis on preventive medicine. The program provides regular physical examinations for members and reminds members when they are due for a physical. The center functions as a one-stop service and referral point to appropriate cooperating physicians. Recipients have their choice of a complete range of physicians associated with the Harvard Medical School and four different cooperating hospitals.

In summary, most professions are facing complex problems of defining who their client is; of discriminating among the needs of immediate, intermediate, and ultimate clients; of resolving conflicts between different parts of the total "client system"; and of determining how to reconcile or integrate the needs of the individual with those of the community or society as a whole.

DEPENDENCE VERSUS INDEPENDENCE OF THE CLIENT A final set of comments that must be made concerns the increasing emancipation of clients and client systems. As organizations increasingly become the immediate clients of professionals, there is a corresponding power shift away from the dependent client who accepts advice in a docile manner toward the aggressive client who tells the professional what to do or "he will find himself another professional." The engineer, architect, lawyer, doctor, and even professor are seeing areas of their autonomy ebb away as organizations become more powerful in dictating what they want the professionals to do. The spectacle, revealed by Ralph Nader, of the suppression or distortion of the findings of a group of government scientists in the Food and Drug Administration (FDA), of industrial research labs finding that products were safe when independent groups had found them unsafe, of architects building antiseptic, unaesthetic office complexes in order to minimize costs, and so on suggests that we must reassess how powerful or autonomous professionals really are in today's organizational society.

The individual client is today more willing to shop around until he finds a doctor, lawyer, or architect who will be responsive to his particular needs; the organizational client is more willing to hire several professionals to work in competition with each other or to hire a second set of professionals to evaluate the work of the first set. Rather than give the architect full control of the project, he will ask him to work as a member of a team with economists, political scientists, planners, and lawyers. More and more middlemen are springing up in the form of consulting firms whose specialty is to help the client define his problem and then find him an appropriate set of professionals to work on it. The consulting firm that has done the initial diagnosis is then in a powerful position to tell the architect just how he should manage the project. The architect cannot use his professional prestige as a lever because he is likely to be dealing with a fellow architect in the planning firm. Increasingly in professions like architecture and engineering, one set of professionals checks on the work of other professionals, forcing the prime designer to be much more explicit about his solutions and giving the client much greater leverage to impose his own constraints. These trends put more pressure on the individual professional and make less clear his precise professional responsibility.

It has been pointed out that professional ethics and standards evolve around the relationship between a professional and a client primarily to protect the client from various forms of malpractice. Such standards are clearest in those areas where there is an unambiguous client and a high risk to the client if the professional service is irresponsible, e.g., medicine. They are least clear where the client is ambiguous and where the risk to the client is not too great (e.g., the engineering work that goes into many consumer products). In the former case there is self-policing by the profession, usually reinforced at the profession's request by legal sanctions. In the latter case—caveat emptor—let the buyer beware and take his risks. In between there is a large area where the client cannot really judge the quality of professional performance but where safety and quality have to reach minimum standards (e.g., the safety of buildings and bridges, the quality of drugs and foods, etc.). In these areas it has been recognized that professional self-policing does not provide sufficient protection to the client, and the federal, state, and local governments have intervened through such agencies as the FDA or through local building codes.

The net effect of these forces is to put the professional more and more on the defensive, tempting him to retreat to the safety of delivering esoteric services only to those clients who wish to purchase them. Thus, while one set of forces is pulling professionals toward more involvement with a wider range of clients, another set of forces is tempting them to retreat to a conservative and safe position. For example, advocacy lawyers, architects, and doctors can sustain this role only as long as there are public funds available and as long as they are perceived to be acting responsibly on behalf of their more ambiguous client systems. As many of these professionals have found, not only do funds run out, forcing them to abandon their new role, but often the very clients whom they are trying to help reject them. The success of the advocacy role thus depends upon having the relevant skills and the protection of a professional role image that is reassuring both to clients and funding agencies.[5]

In summary, as client systems become more differentiated and as clients become more resourceful and powerful, the professions have a less clear concept of what standards and ethics should govern client relationships and are therefore more vulnerable to a variety of attacks and pressures both from their employers and their intermediate and ultimate clients.

---

[5] It has been pointed out that Ralph Nader's success is very much dependent on his being perceived as an extremely responsible person who is using his position to help consumers rather than to become wealthy himself. One of the dangers in the model he is building is that another person could use advocacy law as an instrument for personal gain or for the destruction of organizations which should be preserved but which are too vulnerable to withstand public and legal assaults, e.g., the university.

Each of the changes we have pointed out will put new demands on the professional of the next decade or two. These new demands must be more clearly articulated and new educational forms must be developed to prepare the future professional to respond effectively to them. In the next three chapters we will attempt to sharpen these issues and to identify just what the problem is in professional education.

4. The Changing Needs of Society

Thus far we have focused on a *description* of what the professions are and how they are evolving in response to social changes. We need to look at these changes in somewhat greater detail and to define their impact. This impact is most evident in some of the recent criticisms[1] of professional practice and professional education. These criticisms have come from a variety of sources and have been directed at a variety of professions, notably the helping professions, such as psychiatry and social work, and the professions that have a potential impact on urban problems, such as architecture, law, and teaching.

The criticisms of the professions have been articulated from three basically different perspectives:

1. The perspective of *society*—what functions are the professions intended to fulfill for society? How are these functions changing, and how well are the professions responding?

2. The perspective of the *profession itself*—what trends can one detect that create problems for the practicing professional or the teacher in that profession?

3. The perspective of the *student* who intends to pursue a professional career —what characteristics should the professions display to make rewarding careers possible for talented young men and women, and how could professional education better meet the needs of entrants into the profession?

Let us examine each of these perspectives in turn.

The professions have always played a key role in maintaining the physical, biological, mental, and spiritual health of society. His-

---

[1] Some of the more articulate recent criticisms can be found in Nader, 1969; Schiff, 1970; Wisely, 1970; Zacharias, 1970.

torically, the growth of the professions has been stimulated by the need to develop expert knowledge and expert services in relation to society's major internal and external problems. Medicine and related professions are concerned with the physical health of members of the society; the ministry is concerned with the spiritual well-being of those same members; the teaching and academic professions are concerned with the survival and growth of the culture and values of the society; science and technology are concerned with harnessing the forces of nature to the ends of society, and the development of new knowledge to make economic and social survival more feasible; the law and related professions are concerned with the internal regulation of society to make it a secure place for all of its members; architecture is concerned with key parts of the physical environment and the use of land resources; and the military profession has developed as society's means of protecting itself from others or for expansion into its surrounding environment.

The growth and development of a given profession has been a function of the specific needs to be met and the basic knowledge available to deal with those needs. The criticisms leveled at the professions today mirror these two categories — the professions are seen as insufficiently responsive to some *new* social problems that have been identified, and the professions are seen as failing to take advantage of all the knowledge available to them.

NEW SOCIAL NEEDS   Many of the more pressing problems that face society today are so complex that no *single* profession can ever hope to deal with them effectively. The basic criticism that has been leveled at the professions in this context is that they have failed to develop connections to other professions and have failed to train practitioners in the skills of working collaboratively with other practitioners. It will not be enough for the psychiatrist to collaborate with the social worker or for the architect to work closely with the planner. If the problems of the city, of the environment, of education, of health, and of international relations are to be worked on effectively, we will need to find ways to develop interprofessional teams managed by competent project managers who can weld the various talents of the different professions together into a team effort.

The diversity of talents that will be needed may be illustrated in the area of health. In developing an effective system of health care we will need, beyond the doctor and the nurse and the various paraprofessionals who surround medicine, the efforts of the architect to build more effective health-care facilities, the anthropologist and sociologist to ensure that the facilities and procedures are in line with prevailing cultural values; economists to develop cost-effective health-care systems; lawyers and politicians to make possible the location of health-care centers in places ordinarily used for other purposes (e.g., storefront health centers); engineers to design better automated diagnostic procedures, prosthetic devices, and other mechanical aids; and managers, behavioral scientists, social workers, etc., to help the community develop and effectively utilize the health facilities which are available.

The kinds of interactions between professions and disciplines implied in the above example are duplicated in almost any example one can think of—the control of drugs, the cleaning up of the waterways and air, the development of more effective urban transportation systems, the control of crime and violence, the control of the birthrate, economic development in underdeveloped regions, and so on. In the area of education the problem is apparent in the list of major unsolved problems in the area of education that was generated by the Committee on Basic Research in Education of the National Research Council.

Unsolved Problems	*Relevant Disciplines*
1. *Designing better and more cost-effective school systems*	Psychology, sociology, economics, architecture, political science, law
2. *Reducing conflict between school and community*	Sociology, political science, law, management
3. *Teacher unionization*	Sociology, political science, industrial relations, management, law
4. *Insufficient basic-skill learning, hence unemployable graduates*	Psychology, economics, sociology, guidance counseling
5. *Lack of integration of cognitive, attitudinal, value, and skill components of education*	Psychology, philosophy, sociology
6. *Genetic versus environmental determinants of intellectual level*	Psychology, sociology, anthropology, biochemistry, genetics
7. *Integration of what is taught in the home, through the mass media, and through the schools*	Psychology, sociology, anthropology, political science, communications

The price of progress has been growing complexity and the interdependence of the different segments of society, resulting in social problems of corresponding complexity and interdependence. Yet the professions in general have not been able to look at problems holistically, have not used total-systems concepts, have not identified the interconnections between the areas they are traditionally responsible for, and have not striven to reduce the conceptual boundaries that exist between their underlying disciplines.

TRAINED INCAPACITY

Most of the major professions are now beginning to recognize that they need the ability to work with other professions if they are to respond effectively to the problems of a modern complex society. At the same time, the traditional model of professional education puts so much stress on the professional as an autonomous expert whom the client can trust because of his high degree of skill and high commitment to a professional ethic that we may well have trained out of most of our professionals the attitudes and skills that are needed to work in collaboration with others.

We have built professional schools on a theory of education designed to produce responsible autonomous specialists, and we have encouraged the evolution of a set of professional associations and societies that have, on the whole, attempted to tighten rather than loosen the boundaries of professions. This tightening of the boundaries has been necessary to maintain high standards and, thereby, reassure the public that the profession could indeed be trusted to deliver its service responsibly (Gilb, 1966). The issue facing us today is whether we have in this process also created some real barriers to the development of new *interdisciplinary* professions of the sort that will be increasingly needed in the future. Referring to medical education, Schiff (1970, p. 10) puts the problem as follows:

The rigidity of the post-Flexner medical school curriculum rooted in traditional teaching methods remains. By far the gravest deficiency is not only the lack of curricular bridges across the diverse medical specialties, but across the other key human service disciplines. The growing emphasis on specialization has increasingly parochialized the student physician's training and experience, even prior to his specialty training. By depriving him of an exposure to the breadth of medical practice and problems, and by fostering an early circumscription of professional interest, the current medical school curriculum operates against the need for the student to concern himself with the comprehensive needs of his patient—let alone view such needs as his responsibility. Convincing the senior faculty that courses in public health, community medicine, and comprehensive medical care are critical to the student's training or, at the very least, pertinent to his professional development, has been a difficult task at most medical schools.

Professionals will have to work not only with each other but, as we pointed out in Chapter 3, they will also have to learn how to work more collaboratively with client systems, particularly the ultimate clients or users of the services. As social problems become more complex, it is more difficult for the professional to determine just what the needs of the ultimate client are unless he is willing and able to work with that client and with other professionals in defining those needs. Referring to health-care teams in an inner-city community health agency, Fry and Lech put the issue this way (1971, pp. 22–23):

The implementation of the family-centered approach by the teams, whereby the *total* social-medical needs of an entire family are treated, is another major source of anxiety for the teams. Social problems cannot be ignored. A prescription cannot be given without knowledge of the family's nutritional practices and level of understanding of medicine. Diagnosis of seemingly medical illnesses must include social factors such as the possibility that a mother's pain is symptom of depression from a mental state due to not having the father in the household. The frustration and depression that results from being overwhelmed by these complex issues is reflected in remarks from team members like, "these environmental problems seem to have no solutions," or "around here everything pulls you down, nothing pulls you up."
Often team members are forced to work in relatively new or unknown areas such as a doctor in social welfare problems, FHW's [Family Health Workers] in psychiatric problems, or a nurse in supervision of para-professionals. Such behavior is at odds with the expectation created by prior training and experience. Adjusting to such roles takes time.

Similarly, the architect who is involved in the design of housing systems for the poor cannot succeed if he relies only on his artistic and design skills, since there are too many circumstances — physical and social — that he cannot have empathy for.[2]

Two forces must be overcome if professionals are to become genuinely responsive to clients needs: (1) the pressure toward working primarily with an *elite* clientele, and (2) the tendency to define the client's problems as genetically determined or at least stemming from early youth and hence *fixed*. Most professional training starts with the assumption that the professional will work primarily for those clients who can articulate their needs and who can pay for professional services. Particularly in the training of teachers, social workers, and psychiatrists, the system is geared toward working with clients whose needs fit within a certain defined range and within well-defined "paradigms" (Schiff, 1970). Students or patients whose needs lie outside this range tend to be defined as "crocks" or "special cases" for whom *special* teachers or therapists must be trained. Thus the mainstream of the profession continues to concern itself with the "ideal" clients, while new professions are demanded to deal with the "problem cases." And there is little incentive *within* the profession to reexamine its basic role, its models of professional practice, and its boundaries.

The notion of early or genetic determinism also permits the professional to assume that, if his initial efforts to help do not succeed, it is because the client is unhelpable — he has a limited IQ or lacks motivation or has an inherited disease. Once the professional has defined the client as potentially uneducable or untreatable, there is no longer any incentive to collaborate with him on his problems. The burden is shifted from the shoulders of the professional to the shoulders of the client. Schiff argues that even the concept of *delivery systems,* which imply that all knowledge and skill is in the hands of the professional, should be replaced by the concept of *realization systems,* which utilize the resources of both the professional and the client in creating a solution to the client's problems.

[2] The pressure to work at the large-scale systems level often works counter to the pressure to get more involved with the client. Some architecture students see large-scale designs as a way of affirming their own design skills and really "making a difference"; in order to work collaboratively with community members in helping them redesign their own environment they must abandon the master-plan notion. Doing the former makes the students feel guilty; doing the latter makes them feel impotent. The problem for the architectural profession will be how to develop new models of the architectural process itself that will permit both the architect's and the user's needs to be met.

In summary, it is clear that the training and development of the professional encourage him to see himself as an autonomous expert at a time when society's problems require more collaboration between professional and client and among professionals themselves.

KNOWLEDGE EXPLOSION AND SPECIALIZATION In the last several decades we have witnessed a real explosion in knowledge and technological know-how. Particularly in the scientific disciplines, we have witnessed such dramatic results as sending a man to the moon, synthesizing life in a test tube, and the development of weapons powerful enough to destroy the globe. In this process, most of the traditional disciplines have become so sophisticated and so differentiated into subdisciplines that it is difficult even for the university professor to remain expert in more than a small corner of his field.

This knowledge explosion has three important consequences for the professions:

1 It acts as a strong stimulant to specialization; the task of a generalist in a world in which the knowledge base is getting larger becomes increasingly difficult.

2 It increases the likelihood of early obsolescence; to keep up in one's specialty becomes more difficult as the field changes ever more rapidly, leading either to obsolete forms of practice or greater specialization into even narrower areas.

3 As specialization increases, it becomes harder for professionals to work together on interdisciplinary teams because greater differentiation of fields and specialization leads to sets of attitudes and concepts that can be easily shared only with fellow practitioners in the same or in a related discipline.

The implications are clear—society is generating problems that require interdisciplinary team efforts for their solution and, at the same time, sets of professionals who are less and less able to take part in interdisciplinary problem-solving efforts. This is true in medicine, in law, in psychiatry, in engineering, and in the academic profession itself, where it has been particularly difficult to launch interdisciplinary efforts in an environment dominated by departments built around disciplinary specialties.[3]

[3] Gordon Brown, former dean of MIT's School of Engineering, recently called for a major reorientation of engineering curricula to make them more interdisciplinary (Brown, 1970).

THE COMPEN-SATORY ROLE OF THE APPLIED BEHAVIORAL SCIENCES

In the last two decades there has been considerable growth of knowledge and skill in the *applied* behavioral sciences, particularly in those aspects that deal with the *identification of social problems* and the *changing of organizational systems.* This area has acquired many labels such as "the theory and practice of planned change," "applied behavioral science," "organizational psychology," "interpersonal and group dynamics," "organization development," etc.[4] It has drawn its practitioners from a broad range of disciplines, notably social psychology, clinical psychology, sociology, applied anthropology, adult education, social work, psychiatry, and systems analysis. Scholars and practitioners in this area are beginning to show up in medical schools, law schools, social work schools, schools of architecture and urban planning, and, less frequently, in schools of engineering. The implications of this trend are very important to consider:

1   The *diagnostic skills* essential in assessing the dimensions of a complex social problem and the relevance of different professions to the solution of that problem will probably come from the applied behavioral sciences.

2   The skills needed to *build, train, and manage interdisciplinary teams* of professionals will probably come from the applied behavioral sciences.

3   The skills needed to train professionals to *work collaboratively with clients and with fellow professionals* clearly come from the applied behavioral sciences. If such skills become more relevant and important, certain elements of the applied behavioral sciences will have to be introduced into *all* professional curricula.

4   The stimulus to the *analysis of the value issues* that underlie professional practice and technological developments will increasingly come from the behavioral sciences. Thus, to the extent that we want our engineers, doctors, lawyers, and architects to become more "humanized," we will have to turn for help more to the behavioral sciences and possibly less to the humanities.[5]

5   The behavioral sciences will become more relevant to the *basic science* component of the professional curriculum as connections are discovered

---

[4] See, for example Bennis, Benne, & Chin, 1969; Bennis, 1966, 1969; Miles, 1964; Schein & Bennis, 1965; Schein, 1965, 1969; Beckhard, 1969.

[5] We are not denying the role the humanities have always played in stimulating analysis of value issues but are asserting that the behavioral sciences are becoming more central in this area, particularly because of the pedagogical devices that have been invented by behavioral scientists.

between basic psychology, sociology, anthropology, organization theory, etc., and the central issues facing *all* professions (e.g., Abercrombie, 1966, 1967).

In summary, if the professions are to become more interdisciplinary and if professionals are to become more able to work with clients and with other professionals, they will have to integrate both the applied and basic components of the behavioral and social sciences into the professional education and training.

5. The Profession's Perspective on Itself

Many of the most articulate criticisms of the professions come from professionals who can look at their field from the perspective of their own career and education. Often these critics are faculty members in professional schools who have tried to consolidate their own observations with the criticisms they hear from clients, from graduates, and from current students. On the surface these criticisms are similar to the ones we have already cited, but the professional perspective brings to such criticisms an analytical skill that permits us to look a little below the surface and attempt to identify some of the underlying reasons why things are as they are. At this more analytical level we can identify three trends of maturing professions: they become more *convergent* in their knowledge base and standards of practice, (2) they become more highly *differentiated* and *specialized*, and (3) they become more *bureaucratized and rigid* with respect to the career alternatives they allow.

INCREASING CONVERGENCE Professional knowledge can be thought of as consisting of three elements:

1 An *underlying discipline* or *basic science* component upon which the practice rests or from which it developed

2 An *applied science* or *"engineering"* component from which many of the day-to-day diagnostic procedures and problem solutions are derived

3 A *skills* and *attitudinal* component that concerns the actual performance of services to the client, using the underlying basic and applied knowledge[1]

[1] These three elements do not necessarily develop in the order listed. Often the basic science is stimulated by the applied area. They are listed here in the order in which they are typically taught.

Most professional school curricula can be analyzed in terms of the form and timing of these three elements. Usually the professional curriculum starts with a common basic science core followed by the applied science elements. The attitudinal and skill components are usually labeled "practicum" or "clinical work" and may be provided simultaneously with the applied science components or they may occur even later in the professional education, depending upon the availability of clients or the ease of simulating the realities that the professional will have to face.

Different professions can be distinguished on the basis of the degree to which the basic and applied science components have become convergent, by which we mean the extent to which they have achieved a high degree of consensus on the paradigms to be used in the analysis of phenomena and high consensus as to what constitutes the relevant knowledge base for practice (Kuhn, 1970). Thus, medicine, engineering, and, to a considerable extent, law rest on the convergent basic disciplines, respectively, of anatomy and biochemistry, physics and mathematics, and various legal codes and precedents. In contrast, social work, clinical psychology, and teaching rest on more divergent underlying disciplines such as the various branches of psychology, sociology, and anthropology. In between are a number of professions that rest on *both* convergent and divergent disciplines — psychiatry is based on medicine (convergent) and clinical psychology and sociology (divergent); architecture is based on engineering (convergent) and design (divergent); management derives from economics and mathematics (convergent) and the behavioral sciences (divergent).

The applied sciences and practical skills that professionals must learn can similarly be classified as highly convergent or divergent. Thus, surgery, bridge building, the drawing up of contracts or legal codes, the development of a syllabus and bibliography, the design of a cost-accounting system, etc., are all relatively convergent activities in which a high degree of consensus on methods is possible. On the other hand, the design of a house, the diagnosis and/or treatment of an unusual disease, the conduct of a trial before a jury, the design of a course, the choice of psychiatric or social work therapy, the choice of management style to be used with a certain type of subordinate, or the decision whether or not to undertake a new product venture are all highly divergent activities in which little consensus is possible.

Thus, an important part of the training of a professional is what some sociologists have called "training for uncertainty" (Fox, 1967), which involves attitudinal and emotional components such as maintenance of one's self-confidence even when one does not have a clear answer to the problem, willingness to take responsibility for key decisions that may rest on only partial information, willingness to make a decision under conditions of high risk, the ability to inspire confidence in the client even when operating in an area of high uncertainty, and so on. Many of the subtler aspects of professional education are concerned with these attitudinal and emotional variables. For purposes of this analysis the important point to recognize is that even though the underlying disciplines of the profession may be highly convergent, there will be, in all professions, necessary skills that are highly divergent and will remain divergent so long as the problems requiring professional help continue to have unique and unpredictable elements. Indeed, one of the hallmarks of the professional is his ability to take a convergent knowledge base and convert it into professional services that are tailored to the *unique* requirements of the client system.[2]

The inherent tension between convergent and divergent modes of thinking is exacerbated as the pool of reliable, convergent knowledge grows while society, on the other hand, is creating or legitimating ever more complex problems that require ever more divergent thinking skills. Complicating this is the phenomenon that students in increasing numbers seem to want to solve real problems earlier and earlier in their education. How does one ensure that the student gets a thorough grounding in the convergent underlying disciplines if he wants to get involved in the more divergent activities associated with project work and client contact? Thus, professors in medical school are concerned about student indifference to biochemistry, professors in law school are worried that students will start "clinical" activities before they have learned to think like lawyers, and architecture professors are concerned

[2] It is a fairly common observation that the scholar or research scientist is a poor consultant or practitioner when he first begins this activity. While there are probably many reasons for this, one of the crucial ones is the inability of the scholar/researcher to switch his thinking from the convergent mode primarily required in research to the divergent mode required in applying his knowledge to the particular problems of a client. The scholar consultant too often tries to force the client's problem into a paradigm that the scholar is familiar with (convergent mode) instead of listening to the nuances of the client's problem and understanding it as a first approximation from the point of view of the client in terms of the *client's* categories of thinking (divergent mode).

that the pressure toward social relevance will undermine student motivation to really learn design principles thoroughly. In each case, the concern is that the student will get involved in divergent client-centered project work before he has the basic knowledge with which to work. In each case it is also acknowledged that learning the basic science requires a certain discipline and motivation that may be eroded by the glamour of getting involved in live projects.

The key to this dilemma is to invent curricula that can do a better job of *integrating* the convergent and divergent elements of professional education. Instead of debating whether clinical or basic science work should come first, schools will have to invent a form of education that permits basic science, applied science, and clinical modes to be taught simultaneously in an integrated fashion.[3]

INCREASING SPECIAL- IZATION It is a phenomenon inherent in the development of disciplines that as more knowledge is accumulated, it can only be stored and transmitted by being first differentiated into new subunits of manageable size. This trend can be seen most clearly if one looks at the history of college curricula which started with broad categories like theology, philosophy, and mathematics and gradually divided into the plethora of disciplines and subdisciplines that are available to today's students as possible majors or fields of study. The professions have developed in a similar way from a few "ancient and learned" ones such as theology, law, and medicine to today's mass of professions such as nursing, accounting, dentistry, and librarianship.

Even more important, there has been a differentiation into subspecialties within the major professions. Medicine and law are no longer single professions but umbrella terms for a mass of specialties from which the student must select an area of concentration. Students may have a common core of basic sciences in the first year or so of their professional education, but thereafter they tend to become sorted into various technical specialties. Some of the specialties are as convergent as the basic science core, while others are highly divergent. The medical student who goes into surgery, orthopedics, ENT (ear, nose, and throat), or ophthalmology

---

[3] Such integration is less necessary for the basic researcher. As Kuhn points out, in research one must start with convergent approaches while retaining the ability to think divergently when necessary (Kuhn, 1970). For professional applications, however, integration of the two modes is more important.

remains in a fairly convergent field in contrast to the internist, the pediatrician, and the psychiatrist.[4]

The tension between convergent and divergent specialties is obvious in a divergent profession like management, in which the solutions offered by the convergent management scientist who is basing his thinking on mathematics and the quantitative elements of economics are often directly in conflict with the solutions offered by the more divergent behavioral scientist who is basing his thinking on the psychology and sociology of organizational phenomena. Each is a specialist and is highly trained in his specialty, but each approaches problems in a style totally different from the other. There is every reason to believe that the situation we have been describing will continue and even get worse. We will see the emergence of more and more specialties as well as more new professions combining elements of several subspecialties of present professions.

This trend creates two particular problems for the professions: (1) it will become increasingly difficult for clients to determine to which profession they should go for the solution of their problems; and (2) it will become increasingly difficult to develop an integrated view of broad, complex problems because of the technical jargon, different styles of thinking, and different approaches taken by specialists in different areas.

These problems may best be understood by looking at the manner in which they will have to be solved. To deal with problem 1, the professions will have to stimulate the development of a new kind of general practitioner who can serve as an initial diagnostician to help the client select the appropriate mix of specialists. His membership in the profession may be somewhat marginal, but he will play a key role if professional services are to be readily available. To deal with problem 2, the professions will have to (1) teach specialists something about how to work in team settings with other professionals, and (2) stimulate the development of a new kind of manager/administrator who, like the project manager in industry, can bring together a diverse set of specialists, weld them into an effective working team, and manage the team for the duration of the project.

---

[4] Donald Light (1970) has shown how difficult the first year of residency is for psychiatrists because few of the convergent solutions they have learned in medical school are of much help in managing or curing psychiatric patients in a ward.

The training of this new kind of general practitioner who can work within a profession and across professions and can manage interprofessional teams will require new kinds of curricula which start out as general and interdisciplinary and which do not put special emphasis on specialization (e.g., planning, management, policy sciences, applied behavioral sciences). Some professional consultants are now playing such a G.P. role. For example, the planning consultant works with the client to articulate the client's problem; to determine the mix of sociologists, lawyers, economists, engineers, and architects who are needed for the project; and then to help select *and manage* the actual professional team.

INCREASING BUREAUCRA-TIZATION Bureaucratization and conservatism in the professions result from a complex of forces. As a profession matures, it not only acquires a greater base of convergent knowledge, making greater consensus possible among professionals, but it also tends to protect its boundaries or its areas of jurisdiction by creating professional associations which, through peer-group control, define educational requirements, standards of entry, and ethical standards for practitioners (Moore, 1970; Schiff, 1970). Professional associations normally create autonomy for the profession by imposing tight controls on their own members, thereby reducing public control. Thus licensing laws and similar procedures are usually lobbied for by the profession in order to control their own membership. At the same time, by banding together, the members of the profession can potentially resist the encroachment of the organization that employed them.[5] As Gilb puts it:

Because of the organizational revolution in business, labor, and other fields, and in particular because of the rise of the corporation, doctors and lawyers felt that they would have to organize more effectively or become employees, lose their clients and patients to corporations, or at the very least be forced to accept fees and conditions imposed by third-party intermediaries (1966, p. 35).

[5] In a recent talk, Ralph Nader argued that if scientists and engineers are to be expected to expose their own employers if they discover unethical or unsafe practice, they must receive increasing support from their professional associations (Boffey, 1971). However, as professional associations have grown more powerful, they themselves have become more bureaucratized and therefore less responsive to appeals such as Nader's.

The professionals wanted, in effect, more control over their own work. They felt that their status and power depended on their ability to control the quality and number of persons admitted to the profession and to maintain discipline. The professional wanted to create an abstract standard, enforced by his peers or by the state if necessary, that would guide and hence stand between the individual professional and those who might otherwise have arbitrary power over him (1966, p. 37).

Any system of peer controls will tend to be conservative, because the behavior of any member of the fraternity reflects on the fraternity as a whole. Innovative tendencies that involve any deviance from professional norms will be frowned upon because they threaten the profession's image. This conservatism tends to be strongest in those professions that are still trying to legitimate themselves in the eyes of the public.

At the same time, as periods of professional education become longer, there is more likelihood that the student will be socialized to the present norms of the profession and, therefore, will tend less toward deviant or innovative behavior in the first place. As Gilb (1966, pp. 78–79) points out, this process not only affects standards of practice but the discovery and dissemination of new knowledge as well:

The profession wants and needs to have some peer-group control over the discovery and spread of new professional knowledge. Through this control it protects itself and the public against quackery and facilitates the spread of new professional discoveries once they have been approved. However, this control also implies a measure of restriction, a resistance to new ideas or techniques that might unseat old chieftains or require a radical shift in orientation or jurisdiction.

Through their magazines and journals, scientific and technical conferences and meetings, continuing education programs, and the informal social interchange at association meetings, the collective "mind" of the profession is molded, skills and techniques are developed and transmitted, the limits of the intellectual scope of the profession's knowledge are established, and the avenues in which knowledge might advance are marked out.

Thus, through the growth of professional associations, the profession as a whole gains autonomy but at the same time puts more restrictions on the behavior of the professional.[6] With increasing specialization, each specialty has tended to develop its own professional association. Such associations have attempted to protect their own members from the encroachment of other professionals rather than to solve the problem for the client:

Sometimes members of different professions work together on a common problem, such as lawyers and doctors in malpractice suits, or lawyers and representatives of various professions who serve as expert witnesses, or lawyers and doctors and social workers on adoptions, or lawyers and accountants on business problems. Professional associations help to define their respective roles. One effect of the growth in the size of public structures and the development of a more complex building technology is that architects have to work with other professionals as a team: soil and site, structural, electrical, and mechanical (heating and plumbing) engineers. Architects themselves have urged the adoption of the concept of an aesthetic team that would include landscape architects, interior designers, sometimes painters and sculptors. Wherever two or more professions overlap, there have been jurisdictional disputes and questions of authority relationships. Who shall be the coordinator? Who does the synthesis for the client or patient? The associations try to establish general principles to govern the work relationships involved.

When the problem has not been one of collaboration, but rather competition for work between established professions and new vocational groups, sometimes the former groups have tolerated "encroachments"; sometimes they have reached jurisdictional agreements with the competing groups; more often they have used a variety of devices to combat the encroachment (Gilb, 1966, p. 87).

The problem for the professions, then, is how to stimulate the kind of innovation that will make them responsive to the increasingly complex problems with which society confronts them. Constant subdividing into new specialities and new professions will not solve the problem if each new group itself takes a conservative

[6] Also, as professional associations have grown in size and power, they have increasingly acquired permanent staff members and stable structures of their own: " . . . there is evidence of oligarchy and bureaucracy: long tenure in the more powerful positions; the path to high office at the national level normally through long service in offices at levels below; and positions of power tending to be held by persons of high (but not the highest) prestige and authority within the profession. Further, permanent staff members play an increasingly important role in making or guiding decisions" (Gilb, 1966, p. 128).

view of its role. One form of evolution is from within through "role innovators" (Schein, 1970*b*). These members of the profession accept its central or pivotal norms but try to redefine where, how, and on whom the profession is to be practiced. A strong theme in this group has been the concern for the ultimate client, who is the actual receiver of professional services but who may have little or no voice in the design of those services—the consumer, the low-income tenant, the welfare recipient, the nonpaying charity case in the local hospital, the ghetto dweller. Thus, advocacy law and advocacy architecture are efforts by some lawyers and architects to provide services to clients who never saw themselves as clients, who did not realize that they were entitled to any voice in their own affairs, and who could not pay professional fees. If a profession is to combat some of its tendencies toward bureaucratization and conservatism through the stimulation of role innovators, it must develop an educational process that produces a higher number of such individuals.

A second method of compensating for conservative trends is through the development of new kinds of *inter*professional groups whose norms at the outset encourage interprofessional collaboration, solutions that emphasize maximum concern for the ultimate user, willingness to make complex diagnoses even if these involve jurisdictional problems, and willingness to train collaborative interprofessional teams. The only existing models of such groups are some of the planning or management consulting firms which themselves involve a high degree of collaboration internally—e.g., Arthur D. Little; OSTI; Dober, Paddock & Upton; and the National Training Laboratories—Institute of Applied Behavioral Sciences to name only a few. The employees of such groups either come from highly divergent professions such as management or the behavioral sciences, or, if they are lawyers, doctors, engineers, or architects, have usually taken some additional formal or informal courses in management and/or the behavioral sciences during their early career.

In this chapter we have attempted to analyze three basic trends in the professions: (1) the trend toward increasing convergence in the knowledge and skill base of the profession; (2) the trend toward increasing specialization and consequent fragmentation of the professions into subprofessions and new professions; and (3) the trend toward increasing bureaucratization and tightening of boundaries within each of the professional specialties. These trends run counter to the social trends identified in Chapter 4. As social problems and client needs become more complex, professionals need to become more skilled in integrating convergent and divergent forms of thinking, more able to work across specialties and/or to integrate the efforts of a number of specialists, and more able to invent innovative ways to relate to clients and work on client problems. Given these opposing sets of forces, one can understand why the professions are under tension and why reform of professional education is not a simple or automatic process.

6. The Changing Values and Needs of Students

Student criticisms of professional education and early career training reflect a change in social values and changed expectations about career opportunities. Students, especially, feel that the professions are losing their connection with real social problems. Increasingly young people ask whether the right sets of clients are being served —i.e., is it right that members of higher socioeconomic strata, because of their greater ability to pay high professional fees, receive better medical, psychiatric, and legal care? Is it right that large corporations have better legal advice than the unorganized consumer? Is it right that the architect is more responsive to the cost reduction philosophy of the government or of his corporate employer than to the needs of the consumer for high-quality products? From the perspective of the student, many professionals as individuals and many professional associations have not sufficiently reexamined their role in society, are not delivering a high-quality service to the right client, and are not responsive to the desire of young professionals to work on relevant social problems.

The *second* criticism is closely related to the first—in many professions, the early years of practice are perceived as stultifying, unchallenging, and more like an initiation rite than an educationally useful apprenticeship. There is a growing conflict between the tendency of the professions to tighten their boundaries, *increase* admission standards, and *stiffen* licensing procedures, and the needs of young practitioners to find ways of engaging in challenging, meaningful projects early in their careers. Increasingly, young architects reject the requirement of working for three years as an apprentice as part of the licensing procedure; engineers leave large corporations if their jobs are too circumscribed; lawyers reject law firms which have too rigid an apprenticeship system and seek more exciting ventures like "Nader's Raiders"; and doctors leave medical careers in favor of management training to find a more exciting and relevant career than day-to-day practice.

Third, from the point of view of the student, the rules of entry into professional school and the curriculum itself are often too rigidly structured. This rigidity has a number of elements. Perhaps most salient is the age discrimination for *entry* into school that favors the individual directly out of college or someone with only a *few* years of experience. Only rarely is a school set up to admit someone in his mid-thirties or early forties, even though a growing number of people would like to change careers in midlife, and many of these people would have the requisite talents for professional careers as doctors, lawyers, or ministers (Drucker, 1968).[1] A similar kind of discrimination works against women, especially in midlife.

A second element of rigidity is the *pacing* of the curriculum. In spite of persuasive evidence that different individuals learn at different rates and in spite of the need for special training for the various new professional roles we have described, most school curricula are designed to graduate students in a fixed number of years. Only some Ph.D. programs recognize that different students with different interests may require varying periods of time to successfully complete their dissertation research.

A third element of rigidity is the *fixed sequence*, starting with *a large common core, offering only a few electives or options* in the middle of the program, and ending with clinical or practicum courses. As we have argued, these various curriculum elements need to be better integrated.

Fourth, most professional education makes very few provisions for a smooth transition to professional practice or for the continuing education of practitioners. Once the student has completed his professional education, he is more or less on his own to find the right kind of job and to keep himself up to date by whatever means he can find. He receives some help from professional associations through seminars, meetings, publications, and other professional activities, but he generally loses touch with his school except as an alumnus who is expected to help the school rather than vice versa.

---

[1] As an example of loosening up the professional education structure, MIT has recently received a grant to retrain unemployed scientists and engineers for work on urban problems.

In order to make a smooth transition into practice and to avoid obsolescence, professional education must emphasize "learning how to learn." The emphasis in most curricula is on currently available knowledge; consequently, most graduates suffer from arrested development. They conduct their professional careers on a knowledge base that may be 10 to 20 years behind the times.

Thus the student's development is limited by the knowledge base he acquires. In addition to this, he is often overtrained to look at problems from a given perspective, making him unable to *identify* problems that require other perspectives. Ralph Nader (1969, p. 20), talking about legal education, has labeled this process "education into corridor thinking" and has articulated how the Socratic or case method, as used in law, channels thinking into certain predetermined molds:

Harvard Law's most enduring contribution to legal education was the mixing of the case method of study with the Socratic method of teaching. Developed late in the nineteenth century under Dean Christopher Columbus Langdell, these techniques were tailor-made to transform intellectual arrogance into pedagogial systems that humbled the student into accepting its premises, levels of abstractions and choice of subject. Law professors take delight in crushing egos in order to acculturate the students to what they called "legal reasoning" or "thinking like a lawyer." The process is a highly sophisticated form of mind control that trades off breadth of vision and factual inquiry for freedom to roam in an intellectual cage.

Most professional curricula are only now beginning to recognize the importance of developing an approach to learning which will permit the graduate to continue to learn on his own after he leaves school. Without adequate opportunities to gain self-awareness, the student cannot learn how to diagnose his own or others' needs except in a mechanistic manner; nor will he be able to take into account his own biases in applying his professional skills. There is ample evidence that personal biases do enter into professional decisions to a considerable extent, even in the more technical, impersonal professions, suggesting that, rather than demanding that professionals be "objective," we should help students to learn how their own personality interacts with their approach to the diagnosis and treatment of client problems. The emphasis that psychiatric residencies place on the resident's personal therapy should be mirrored in other professions through the development of more personally oriented learning experiences (Light, 1970; Abercrombie, 1967).

Finally, most students are faced with the reality that obtaining the economic and status rewards normally associated with being a professional will require of them an adherence to norms and standards set by professional associations, and that those norms and standards are likely to push them into a high degree of specialization, forcing them to be less and less responsive to some of the problems that brought them into the profession in the first place. The price of professional status has often been the giving up of the creative urge or the urge to work on more socially relevant problems.[2]

The above points have been dramatized and, perhaps, exaggerated. Many of the more innovative schools do not have the rigidities that have been described. Many professions recognize these rigidities and are working to overcome them. But student dissatisfaction is currently at a high enough level that we must question whether the present rate of change is sufficient.[3]

In this chapter we have tried to show how some of the needs and values of students reinforce many of the criticisms previously discussed. The professions thus find themselves squeezed from both directions—by society via changing clients and changing client needs, and by students entering the professions with new values, different aspirations, and more varied career goals. The pressure is perhaps strongest within the professional schools themselves because of the immediacy of student demands and the ideological commitment of schools to being responsive and responsible.

The first six chapters of this book have attempted to lay out some of the structural characteristics of the professions and some of the major criticisms that have been leveled at the professions. We have tried to show how these criticisms have resulted from an incongru-

[2] For a good example of how this process works in medical school, the reader should consult Becker et al., 1961.

[3] "A meeting was held recently in Washington, of a group that calls itself 'The Architects Resistance' whose purpose, as now described, is to work out a whole new mode of creating architecture, or designing environments. The members are young, and the movement was orginally formed to protest specific actions that they felt were immoral, such as designing buildings in South Africa, or a firm designing a new building that would displace large numbers of poor people from a ghetto area. Not a lot was decided, except to try to start some sort of communication medium to connect people across the country" (Steele, personal communication, May 1970).

ence between the changing needs and values of society on the one hand and the natural course of development of the professions on the other. It is crucial to understand this incongruence, because it explains the slow rate of change within the professions and within professional schools.

7. New Directions for Professional Education

In this chapter we will move from a description of the existing state of affairs to some conclusions on new directions for professional education. First we will recapitulate the basic criticisms of the professions that come from society, from professionals themselves, and from students entering the profession. Having restated these, we will indicate some of the directions that professional education should take, noting in that process the basic difficulties that will be encountered in making such changes.

SUMMARY OF CRITICISMS OF THE PROFESSIONS The criticisms of the professions and of professional education tend to be the same, whether from the perspective of society, of the professions themselves, or of students entering the professions. They can be summarized as follows:

1 The professions are so specialized that they have become unresponsive to certain classes of social problems that require an interdisciplinary or interprofessional point of view—e.g., the urban problem.

2 Educational programs in professional schools, early career paths, and formal or informal licensing procedures have become so rigid and standardized that many young professionals cannot do the kind of work they wish to do.

3 The norms for entry into the professions have become so rigid that certain classes of applicants such as older people, women, and career switchers are, in effect, discriminated against.

4 The norms of the professions and the growing base of basic and applied knowledge have become so convergent in most professions that it is difficult for innovations to occur in any but the highly specialized content areas at the frontiers of the profession.

5 Professionals have become unresponsive to the needs of many classes of ultimate clients or users of the services, working instead for the organization that employs them.

6 Professional education is almost totally geared to producing autonomous specialists and provides neither training nor experience in how to work as a member of a team, how to collaborate with clients in identifying needs and possible solutions, and how to collaborate with other professionals on complex projects.

7 Professional education provides no training for those graduates who wish to work as members of and become managers of intra- or interprofessional project teams working on complex social problems.

8 Professional education generally underutilizes the applied behavioral sciences, especially in helping professionals to increase their self-insight, their ability to diagnose and manage client relationships and complex social problems, their ability to sort out the ethical and value issues inherent in their professional role, and their ability to continue to learn throughout their career.

POSSIBLE DIRECTIONS OF REFORM OR INNOVATION Most analyses of professional education, indeed most analyses of higher education in general, start with a set of problems or criticisms such as those listed above and then make a series of recommendations about needed changes. Since we are assuming that there are strong restraining forces or barriers operating, we will not make recommendations as such but rather state some directions toward which professional education should move. Having identified these directions and some of the difficulties of getting there, we will then describe a change model and some mechanisms that may facilitate movement toward the new educational forms and emphases that will be required in professional schools.

Direction 1. More flexibility in the professional school curriculum, in the number of paths available through the school, in the number of electives available to students inside and outside the school, in the pacing and sequencing of courses, in the required length of time needed to go through school, and in the degree or certification process used by the school

The reasons for this direction are obvious in terms of the problems we have previously identified. Women with family commitments or people who are preparing for career switches or who want to pursue a professional education sometime after college would benefit from the kind of flexibility that would permit them to obtain a degree through part-time study. In such cases, economic motivation may be a factor if the person (1) could not afford to go earlier, or (2) recognizes the added value of professional education, or (3) takes advantage of a tuition refund plan offered by his employer. He or she may also be motivated by genuine changes in values and interests such as those exhibited by an increasing number of engineers and managers who wish to become doctors, lawyers, or ministers.

The obvious problem in moving toward a more flexible curriculum is that the body of knowledge in a profession is growing and is regarded by most professionals as a required core to be learned by all students as part of their basic education in the profession. Closely correlated with this core growth is the norm in most professions that competence requires a high degree of motivation and dedication that must be manifested fairly early in life. People who want to study part-time, women who are concerned about the family, and people who want to switch careers or return to school later are almost automatically suspected of lack of motivation and dedication. Hence admissions committees typically argue that they would rather admit a highly motivated 21-year-old who wants to study full-time than a 40-year-old part-time student whose motivation is suspect. Such arguments are bolstered by horror stories of the older or part-time student who was admitted and turned out to lack competence or motivation and thus wasted everyone's time.

In the present climate of cost cutting in education there is a further force against creating flexible programs: elective courses tend to cost more because a larger faculty is needed to teach both a required program and an elective program. If the electives are taken outside the school, the cost to the professional school does not go up, but the cost to the university as a whole does go up in that the departments offering the electives (typically humanities or social science departments) look unfavorably on the costs of teaching "out-of-course students" unless the university reimburses the department for such "service" courses. One solution to such pressure is to let classes get larger. This solution saves faculty time but pushes the school toward a lecture-recitation system that violates other desirable directions of change. In my experience, the economic arguments always loom very large when reforms or innovations are suggested because the innovator is typically unable to demonstrate in any convincing fashion that his new approach would be cheaper or at least no more expensive than the present approach.

Many schools in their legitimate efforts to better understand the

costs of education have adopted cost-accounting models or information and control models that have been developed for business and
industry. What such models often reveal is the high cost of electives
and flexible curriculum plans because the models are typically
built around measures of faculty-student contact hours. Required
courses are automatically larger and are therefore most cost-effective by this measurement system. What is missed in this system is
a measure of student motivation, involvement in the course, and
amount of useful knowledge or skill learned. If we had better
measures of amount learned, we might find that smaller courses
and elective courses have greater impact because they maximize
student motivation and involvement.

In summary, though it seems clear that professional education
needs to become more flexible in a number of respects, there are
very powerful forces built into the present system which, if anything, will make education *more uniform.* Efforts toward flexibility have been made in some schools but they are dramatic exceptions at this point.

Direction 2. More flexibility in the early career paths of professionals, more differentiated rules for licensing to reflect different
kinds of professional careers, and more support by the profession
itself of role innovation of various kinds

To recapitulate, we have noted the rapidly changing kinds of
problems society is generating for professionals to work on, the
rapidly changing pattern of employment settings within which
professionals work, the correlated changes in the clientele and
client systems to which professionals must relate, the growing
need for a new "general practitioner" who can help clients locate
the right mix of specialists, and the growing need for managers of
professional teams.

If the flexibility implied by direction 1 begins to take shape, it
must be supported by comparable flexibility in early career paths
and systems for licensing and rewarding professional performance
that may lie outside the mainstream of professional practice. Such
flexibility must have the support not only of the professions but
also of employers and other financers of professional services.
Without such a total approach, there is the great risk that new
curricula will encourage many young professionals (e.g., architects)
to work on urban problems and to become expert in this area at a

time when money to support urban projects runs out. As we indicated above, a number of young architects are now in a reluctant and somewhat embittered way forcing themselves to go back to more traditional private and corporate clients to make a living.

The obvious problem in creating more flexible career paths is that the very existence of such paths poses a threat to the traditional practitioner in that it forces him to at least consider the possibility that his own career style is no longer in the mainstream and, indeed, may even be obsolete. A correlated problem is that, as we have noted, the trend in all professions is toward more specialization and more esoteric uses of the specific pieces of knowledge that basic research is uncovering. Thus the typical trend is to ask of each young practitioner that he learn *all* the basic core of the profession *plus all* the detail of a chosen specialty. There is little support in the norms of most professions for careers that put more emphasis on being a generalist and/or being a manager of professional teams.

A further restraining force on loosening up career paths is that for most professions the process of legitimating themselves with the public has involved carving out some easily described areas of practice and surrounding those areas of practice with strong, self-imposed regulations for entry into the profession and licensing of performance. The newer areas of role innovation are harder to describe, more vulnerable to unprofessional self-seeking or outright charlatanism, and hence harder to legitimate with the public. How then can one ensure responsibility? The usual answer is "by having the person first go through the traditional curriculum and apprenticeship" that presumably inculcates the high ethical standards needed of a professional person. Whether or not this answer is in fact correct, the *issue* of how to build a strong sense of responsibility remains, and many professionals will argue that only a *standard* curriculum and *standard* early career will ensure it.

Finally, many of the new career paths will involve crossing professional boundaries by putting together skills that come from more than one profession. Such careers will create further problems of legitimation. For example, should a project manager of an architectural team that is building a large urban housing project be legitimated by architects, by managers, or by both? At the present stage in the development of the professions, we do not have models of how to solve jurisdictional problems like these or how to license individuals with cross-professional skills.

In summary, as in the case of creating more flexible curricula, we can identify in the case of creating more flexible early career paths some real restraining forces or barriers that derive from the nature of the professions themselves. In particular, a mechanism will have to be found for reassuring potential clients that individuals in role-innovative careers are competent and responsible.

Direction 3. New curricula and new career paths which are inter- or transdisciplinary and which may lead eventually to new professions that have new blends of knowledge and skill underlying them

The basic reason for such a development is that increasingly the problems of society require inter- or transdisciplinary skills for their solution. Most discussions of this issue do not differentiate the *several meanings which are implied by the term* interdisciplinary:

Meaning 1 A curriculum that involves *courses from two or more departments or disciplines* leading to a degree named after one of them, or a degree "without specification." Thus, at MIT, a student who wishes to go into "educational management" can take some courses at Harvard's School of Education, some behavioral science and management courses at MIT's Sloan School, write his thesis about an innovative program for teaching freshman science at MIT, and receive a Ph.D. from MIT without a specific disciplinary name attached to it.[1] Or a student wishing to design a better braille system or better prosthetics for paraplegics may take some courses in electrical engineering, some courses in mechanical engineering, some courses in the biology department, and some courses in the psychology department leading to a degree in biomedical engineering. A graduate version of this program is now being developed that allows students to combine engineering courses at MIT with medical courses at the Harvard Medical School.

Meaning 2 A curriculum that involves *several disciplines, all of which are located within a given school.* Thus, in most management schools students have to take courses in economics, psychol-

---

[1] A program such as this would be administered by the Graduate School and by a committee consisting of faculty members from both schools.

ogy, quantitative methods, and various applied areas like finance, production, industrial relations, and marketing. In most medical schools, students take not only the courses directly relevant to medicine but also additional work in sociology, anthropology, or some other behavioral science. Law schools are beginning to add political science, economics, and sociology to the traditional law courses. Architecture and engineering schools are beginning to recognize the relevance of other disciplines but have not yet introduced them in a major way.

Meaning 3 Schools that are from the outset interdisciplinary or transdisciplinary in their orientation in that they set as their goal *the development of a new discipline that represents an integration of the disciplines represented.* As yet there are not many examples of this model, though a growing number of schools of "policy sciences" attempt to integrate economics, political science, behavioral science, law, and management into a single coherent discipline.[2] Similarly, some schools of management attempt to integrate economics, behavioral science, and quantitative methods into a single discipline of management. Sometimes such schools arise out of research- and applications-oriented *centers* that are initially organized to deal with some important practical problem. For example, out of our concern for environmental quality may come some new disciplines and new professions which combine sociology, political science, engineering, and management. The product may be an "environmental doctor" whose skills will lie in the ability to diagnose a problem and work with the community in solving it. The profession of consultant may be divided into two broad categories on this basis: some are technical specialists (the pathology consultant in medical diagnosis), and others are generalists, having integrated a number of disciplines relevant to a practical problem (the management consultant or planning consultant).

It is our impression that what is needed is more of the *third* kind of transdisciplinary effort, yet what most schools advertise reflects the first meaning, with an occasional effort to move into the second type of program. The reasons for this trend are not hard to discern. The very nature of learning a discipline is a process of moving deeper and deeper into a given way of thinking, using the

---

[2] The most recent example is the Policy Sciences Program at the State University of New York at Buffalo, started by Warren Bennis.

vocabulary and concepts of that discipline. Competence in the discipline is typically defined as the ability to work at the frontiers of that discipline, which requires deep involvement and thorough understanding. Professors, who are intellectually immersed to that degree, may find it difficult to understand another discipline at anything but a superficial level or to empathize with each others' concepts and perspectives on theory, research, and even teaching methods. Thus, integrating several disciplines is extremely difficult at best, even when these disciplines are clearly relevant to an important problem area.

If one looks at transdisciplinary *research,* one finds many examples of the model 1 or model 2 kind of interdisciplinary effort (i.e., professors from several disciplines working *side by side* on a common problem) but very few integrated efforts in which each professor is in some real sense *dependent* upon another one. By *interdependence* we mean something like an endocrinologist working with a behavioral scientist to determine the behavioral effects of changing hormone levels, a surgeon working with a behavioral scientist on the differential effects of different kinds of brain lesions, or an architect working with a lawyer in implementing an urban housing project. Recent efforts by granting agencies such as the National Science Foundation to increase transdisciplinary research are as yet difficult to evaluate, but it is our prediction that many transdisciplinary proposals that promise the model 3 type of integration will, in fact, end up with a model 1 or model 2 parallel interdisciplinary research program.

Many interdisciplinary programs or schools fail to integrate the disciplines at the level of the faculty or the curriculum, but the students who come out of such programs often do have a more integrated view. This is evident in management, where those Ph.D. students who have majored both in finance and in behavioral science have a more integrated view of organizations and can both teach and do research in terms of this more integrated view. However, when it is time for those young professors to work in a school of management, they find themselves back in a department that contains mostly colleagues from one discipline or the other, making it difficult for them to sustain their integrated approach. If they have worked for a period of years on applied problems that *required* the transdisciplinary integrated view, they are likely to have published papers that do not appeal to their more discipline-oriented colleagues and thus find it difficult to return to the professorial ranks.

In summary, given the nature of disciplines and the typical organization of professional schools, it is an inherently difficult task to achieve transdisciplinary integrated curricula. Such curricula will not emerge until we find ways of getting professors or practitioners from different disciplines to recognize areas of interdependence and thus to become motivated to learn each others' concepts, perspectives, and working styles.

Direction 4. Complete integration of the behavioral and social sciences into the professional school curriculum at three different levels: (1) basic psychology, sociology, anthropology, and economics as part of the basic science core of professional education; (2) applied behavioral science dealing with the theory and practice of planned change, diagnosis of complex systems, and analysis of client-professional relationships; and (3) applied behavioral science dealing with self-insight, social responsibility, learning how to work in and lead professional teams, and learning how to learn

Most professionals need a thorough understanding of human behavior at the individual, group, organizational, and societal levels if they are to deliver their service effectively. This has always been recognized in professions like psychiatry, social work, and management, but it is only recently being recognized in engineering, architecture, law, medicine, and other professions that have a more convergent technical core. For example, architects are beginning to understand the relevance of psychology to understanding their own and their clients' perceptual processes and how these processes affect the use of different kinds of designs, the relevance of sociology and anthropology to understanding the forces that act in a city, and how symbolic meanings deriving from cultural norms influence the perception and use of physical space.[3] The particular blend of behavioral and social sciences that is relevant to any given profession will vary with the basic nature of that profession, but it is becoming clearer that every professional needs some exposure to these disciplines as part of his basic science education.

Moving to the second level of use, it is becoming clear that as the work settings, the client systems, and even the nature of the professional services shift with the growing complexity of society, it

[3] For recent work in this area, the reader should consult Abercrombie (1960, 1967), Sommer (1969), and Steele (in press).

is more important for the professional to learn something about how to diagnose social systems, complex human relationships, and change problems. We are dealing here less with a basic science component and more with an applied skill that is relevant to the day-to-day practice of the professional. Such a skill will become more and more relevant as professionals find themselves increasingly dealing with complex client systems in which the service to be delivered is part of a long-range change process. The theory and practice of planned change has been developed in a number of disciplines and can now be taught in a coherent fashion.

The third level of use of the behavioral sciences involves a number of components that are of increasing importance to all professionals. First of all, it is clear that the client-professional relationship is sufficiently complex that any professional (not just the psychiatrist) must have a certain amount of self-insight, knowledge of the consequences of his own decisions, and some sense of social responsibility relative to those decisions. For example, the architect must realize how much power he may have over a client, how little the client will be able to articulate his own needs, and how much, therefore, the client's ultimate welfare will depend upon design decisions that the architect makes unilaterally. If the project is a large-scale urban redevelopment, the consequences of the architectural decisions may involve thousands of people for very long periods of time. Similarly, the engineer designing products must become aware of the consequences of his design decisions for the consumer and, ultimately, for society.

The traditional solution to the problem of building self-awareness and a sense of social responsibility has been to increase the humanities portion of the curriculum. There is growing evidence, however, that whatever other value the humanities may have, they have *not* been very successful in stimulating the growth of self-insight and of a sense of the value issues inherent in any profession. When one looks at the kinds of courses taught in humanities and the teaching methods that are used, it becomes clear that the relationship between professional practice and social policy is rarely touched upon. On the other hand, applied behavioral science workshops and seminars dealing with "here and now" kinds of behavior and issues have been successful in stimulating the growth of self-insight and have led people to examine their own value systems and the relationship of their own behavior to values and social policies.

A related goal of this third level of application would be to stimulate learning how to learn, enabling the student to develop his own capacities to determine what he needs to know and how to go about learning those things without the formal supports of a school and a curriculum. If he does not acquire these skills, he is in great danger of becoming technologically obsolete within a few years after graduation or, worse, of continuing to practice in terms of a knowledge and skill base that is no longer relevant to the problems he is trying to solve.

A third goal of this application level of applied behavioral science would be to teach the skills of working collaboratively with others in professional teams and to play leadership and managerial roles in such teams when needed. Such skills are best learned through the same kinds of seminars and workshops as those designed to increase self-insight; hence they have been lumped together here. Workshops that last from one to three weeks could involve groups of students in exploring their own functioning, the consequences of their behavior, the relationship of their behavior to values, how to work with other people, and how to play useful leader roles in teams.

The barriers to the introduction of the behavioral and social sciences at all these levels are considerable. First, there is the lack of awareness of professional school faculties of what parts of psychology, etc., are relevant to their curriculum. Second, many professions have a negative stereotype of the applied behavioral sciences as manipulative. To face the issue of manipulation would force the professional to look at his present ways of influencing others, and one senses that such self-analysis is inherently threatening, especially to engineers, architects, doctors, and lawyers. Third, the applied behavioral sciences are probably directly threatening to those professionals who have entered a field because their motivation was to avoid having to work closely with people, e.g., engineering (Davis, 1965; Perrucci & Gerstl, 1969). Fourth, the behavioral sciences are seen as too seductive, pulling the student away from the basic knowledge and skill he is supposed to acquire in his profession. One suspects that the demise of sensitivity training groups in some architecture schools resulted partly from the fact that students became too interested in themselves and less interested in learning the basics of architectural design. If indeed the last-named barrier is a significant one, it suggests that the timing of applied behavioral science activities becomes a crucial determinant of whether or not they will be acceptable.

Insofar as the theory and practice of planned change lies presently within the domain of the behavioral sciences, it will be their own burden to devise ways of overcoming the resistances to their own utilization. We cannot blame professional schools for underutilizing something whose utility they do not fully understand. We can only strive to make the utility of the behavioral and social sciences more visible and invent ways of introducing them into professional education in a manner that will be less threatening.

In summary, we have identified four directions of change for professional education: (1) more flexible professional schools that permit a variety of paths through the school leading to a variety of careers within the profession; (2) more flexible early career paths which stimulate role innovation and which enable and enhance the variety of career paths launched in professional schools; (3) more transdisciplinary curricula that integrate several disciplines into new professions that will be more responsive to the new social problems of today's and tomorrow's society; and (4) complete integration of the behavioral and social sciences into professional curricula at the basic science and applied skill level.

Part Two
The Prescription

You can't get there from here.

Colloquial

Sir, I'm trying to get to Fryeburg and I see there are two roads from here; which one do I take?

Well, you can take the road up there and it will take you to Fryeburg, and you can take the road down there and it will take you to Fryeburg, too.

Does it make any difference which one I take?

Not to me, it don't.

"Travelling in Maine," anecdote told by Richard Beckhard

It is one thing to identify the forces that are acting on the professions and to make recommendations for changes in professional education; it is another to actually influence the educational practices of professional schools toward the changes that are recommended. Many efforts at educational change or reform still operate by the archaic model that once ideas or facts are published, they will be noted and acted upon. We know that this model is not true even within the domain of the hard sciences, where the diffusion of ideas is a remarkably slow and erratic process. When dealing with a conservative system like the professions, it is even more unlikely that a written analysis will have much impact. Given this pessimistic view, how do we get there from here? How do we stimulate more interdisciplinary professional practice, more collaborative work among professionals, more role flexibility in practitioners, more concern for ultimate users, more collaboration with client systems, more skillful diagnosis of complex social problems and client systems, and more career flexibility in the professions?

We will first describe what we consider a realistic model of how planned change actually occurs (Chapter 8). This model will help us to identify *specific change targets* which will start a change process but which also allow for resistance to change and reformulation of the ultimate goals of change along the way. Secondly, the model will help us identify particular *points of entry* in the professional school system, thus enabling the change agent to think in much more concrete terms about where to start and with what goals (Chapter 9). Ultimately, it will become evident that one cannot *force* change toward a predetermined set of goals, but one can start a change process and manage that change process in a way that will ensure that the ultimate goals are continuously reexamined and that intermediate steps toward them make sense *to the participants* in the change process. Having reviewed the change model in Chapters 8 and 9, we will then present some of the mechanisms that may be tested by professional schools trying to achieve the change goals indicated. Chapter 10 will describe mechanisms now in existence; Chapter 11 will suggest some new mechanisms for a more utopian kind of professional school.

The model we will describe puts heavy emphasis on the involvement and participation of the members of the school or organization that is changing. We can attempt to describe such a model and give some illustrations of how it is applied, but, ultimately, any given school that is intrigued by these ideas will have to go through *its own* diagnostic process and will have to enlist the help of internal and/or external change agents in formulating its change program.[1]

___

[1] For further literature on the theory and practice of planned change, the reader may wish to consult the material mentioned in Chapter 4, footnote 4.

8. A Model of the Process of Planned Change

Professional education can be changed by a deliberate yet controlled process. We do not have to rely on the slow process of evolution, nor would it be appropriate or desirable to have a more drastic revolutionary kind of educational reform. We seek a process that lies somewhere between these two extremes and that has worked well in the transformation of a variety of other kinds of organizations. The particular relevance of *planned* change derives from the fact that we are dealing with organizational change in a setting where there are strong forces opposing the change. We do not mean, however, that changes should be imposed on the professional schools. Our concept of planned change implies a heavy involvement of the organization in the planning of its own change programs.

Planned change involves the learning of new *concepts and ideas,* new *attitudes and values,* and new patterns of *behavior and skills.* Part of any planned change model must therefore be a model of how individuals in a social system *learn* and thereby transform the social system. This learning has to occur in a situation in which, by virtue of their membership in the social system, individuals already have ways of thinking, feeling, and acting to which they are committed and which make sense to them. Such sense may be based on rational diagnosis or may derive from a set of rationalizations for emotionally based traditions or habits. In either case, however, the change agent must assume that the members of the system will be committed to their present ways of operating and will, therefore, resist learning something new. As a consequence, the *essence* of a planned change process is the *unlearning* of present ways of doing things. It is in this unlearning process that most of the difficulties of planned change arise.

We will present a model at three levels of generality—first, an overview model of the process viewed in learning-theory or attitude-change theory terms; second, a specific model of how to identify change needs and change targets, called "force-field analysis," which is designed to be used jointly by the change agent and the person or persons desiring to make changes; and third, an even more specific diagnostic model which helps identify specific points of entry to initiate the change process.

A GENERAL CHANGE MODEL This overview model (Figure 1) was first developed in an effort to understand the attitude changes that took place in civilian and military prisoners of the Chinese Communists in the 1950s (Schein, 1961). The model is an extension of the dynamic-change model developed by Kurt Lewin in the 1940s (Lewin, 1947). Since then the model has been applied to personal change generally (Schein, 1968*b*) and to the process of learning that occurs in human relations laboratories or sensitivity training programs (Schein & Bennis, 1965). As we will see, the steps in the model apply just as well to members of educational systems.

FIGURE 1   *A model of planned change*

Stage 1:	*Unfreezing:*	Creation of the motivation to change
	Mechanisms:	(1) Lack of confirmation or disconfirmation of present beliefs, attitudes, values, or behavior patterns
		(2) Induction of "guilt-anxiety" by comparison of actual with ideal states
		(3) Creation of psychological safety by the reduction of threats or removal of barriers to change
Stage 2:	*Changing:*	Developing new beliefs, attitudes, values, and behavior patterns on the basis of new information obtained and cognitive redefinition
	Mechanisms:	(1) Identification with a particular source of information and redefinition through perceiving things as the source perceives them
		(2) Scanning multiple sources of information and redefinition through new integration of information
Stage 3:	*Refreezing:*	Stabilizing and integrating new beliefs, attitudes, values, and behavior patterns into the rest of the system
	Mechanisms:	(1) Integrating new responses into the total personality or culture
		(2) Integrating new responses into ongoing significant relationships and into total social system through reconfirmation by significant others

It should be noted that if a change program is to be successful, it must pay particular attention to stages 1 and 3. It is not enough just to develop and publish new ideas and to expect that others will take them up, or to give vivid examples and hope that others will, through identifying themselves with our situation, see the relevance of the example and then adopt it. Many innovative ideas in education are never attended to because there is no motivation to change in the first place, and many that are attempted fail to survive because they are not integrated into the total system of the school or the personality of the teacher trying out the innovation. It should also be noted, however, that the term *refreezing,* or integration, does not imply a permanent solution, since new unfreezing forces are always operating. The model should be viewed as cyclical and dynamic. Having given particular emphasis to the importance of stages 1 and 3, let us look at each stage in turn and examine its implications for inducing changes in professional education.

Stage 1: Unfreezing In the first six chapters of this book we have described a number of forces that can be assumed to be acting as unfreezing forces on the professions generally and on professional schools in particular. Professionals in increasing numbers have found that present ways of conducting their daily practice fail to be confirmed[1] or are actually disconfirmed by various client behaviors and by critiques of the professions. Nader has also pointed out how doctors, lawyers, and scientists are failing to live up to the *traditional* ideals of their professions, and students and young practitioners of the advocacy school have called in increasing numbers for the development of *new ideals* in the professions. It is not clear, however, that, simultaneously with this increased pressure to change, there has been a corresponding increase in psychological safety that would make it possible for people to change.

This point is absolutely crucial: *no matter how much pressure is put on a person or social system to change through disconfirmation and the induction of guilt-anxiety, no change will occur unless the members of the system feel it is safe to give up the old responses and learn something new.* Without a feeling of psychological safety, the members of the system will increase in defensiveness in direct

---

[1] The term *confirmed* in this context means that the results of the person's behavior led to expected and desired outcomes.

proportion to the amount of pressure brought to bear. We can see many examples of this mechanism operating in professional school faculties: new program ideas will not be tried because faculty members are afraid that students will learn less or be hurt by a new approach, or because they are unsure unless someone else has already tried it and can reassure them that it will work, or because they are reluctant to expose their fear of not being able to use the new idea effectively (e.g., computer-aided instruction). Fears will often be rationalized in terms of economic arguments ("the innovation will be too expensive") or in terms of attributing problems to some other groups ("students won't know how to cope with that innovation"). In all these cases one must consider the possibility that what the person is really saying is that *he* personally is feeling threatened and/or does not see how to get there from here, hence he tends to resist on an emotional level and develop rationalizations for the resistance.

The essence of an effective unfreezing process is therefore a proper balance of (1) disconfirming forces that do arouse discomfort, tension, and threat, and (2) forces that create sufficient psychological safety to make it possible for the person to pay attention to the disconfirming cues and develop a motivation to change rather than resist change. Too many change processes have come to naught either because there was not sufficient disconfirmation to make members in the system want to change, or because there was so little psychological safety that members in the system had to misinterpret or deny the validity of the disconfirming cues.

If professional education is to change, the change agents[2] working within a particular school must take careful note of the forces operating toward unfreezing the system, and, in particular, they must create a climate in which faculty and administration feel enough psychological safety to see how to overcome the barriers in implementing an innovation. The details of how such a climate is achieved will vary from one person to another and one system to another; hence no *common* prescription can be given. However, we will, in the next chapter, describe a *process* that will help identify barriers and threats in any given change situation.

---

[2] The term *change agent* can refer to a single person or group operating inside or outside the system to be changed. It can be a dean, a professor, a student, a consultant, a committee, or any group that sets as its target the production of change.

Stage 2: Changing Changed cognitions, attitudes, values, and behavior patterns result ultimately from acquiring new information that helps to redefine the situation and thus enables new kinds of responses to be made. The function of unfreezing is to make it possible for the person or system to pay attention to new information that is available. That is, until there is a real motivation to change combined with a sense of psychological safety, the person or system will simply ignore new ideas or deny their validity. Once there is motivation to change, the person or system will search out new ideas and new information in order to develop new attitudes and responses that will be rewarded or confirmed.

The process of searching out occurs in one of two ways: (1) seeking a model with which to *identify,* e.g., another teacher who is teaching in a different way or looking for a school system that is trying an innovation that looks promising or imitating a school that is similar to the one trying to change; or (2) *scanning* the entire information environment and selecting from that environment ideas that best fit the person or system trying to change. Of course, both processes may be used, but it is important to distinguish them because they have different consequences for stage 3 (refreezing).

Identification, the process of locating a single information source and relying primarily on it, is a simple, quick way to find new ideas, attitudes, and behavior patterns; e.g., if Harvard or MIT adopt a new approach to science education, it is easy for other universities to copy that approach. However, an approach that fits Harvard or MIT may simply not be congruent with the culture of the imitator school, hence it may not survive as an innovation. *Scanning,* the process of surveying the environment for a whole range of ideas and attempting to combine them into a package that fits the school's unique situation, will take longer, but is more likely to produce a solution that will be readily refrozen, i.e., integrated into the present system.

What makes most change processes so hazardous is that we typically do not even consider stage 3 — the long-run survival and integration of the innovation — at the time we are inventing new approaches. Often we simply select a source with which to identify and adopt that approach, only to find some years later that the approach must be abandoned because it is not congruent with other elements in the social system. For example, new curriculum packages that are built on assumptions of a more active, involved learner often fail to survive if they are inserted into a school system that is strongly built on assumptions of a passive learner, a system supported by a cadre of teachers who have invested most of their lives in a teaching approach that also presumes more passive learners. These teachers will neither understand nor be able to use effectively the new curriculum packages, often erroneously blaming the package itself for the problem.

If the change agent has reason to believe that certain innovations will not fit the culture of the system that is trying to change, he should encourage members of the system to scan until they find innovative ideas that fit their particular needs and culture and should actually discourage imitation of other systems which seem to have solved the problem but which have different cultures to start with.[3]

This line of thinking can best be illustrated by considering one of the major sources of resistance to change in professional education: the culture and norms of the *academic* profession. Among the key norms that we have mentioned repeatedly is that professionals must learn to be autonomous and to value autonomy. This norm applies especially to professors. Consequently, unless the norm itself is changed, only those innovations that faculty members have invented or selected for themselves will be genuinely integrated into the curriculum.

If the professorial sense of autonomy further extends to the notion that it is the professor's *duty* to teach students those elements of the profession that he, the professor, knows to be necessary for successful performance in that profession, he will automatically resist a whole class of innovations that call for more collaboration between student and teacher in the selection of curriculum content and style of learning. Furthermore, if the professor himself, through the manner in which he conducts the classroom, sets a strong example of *one-way* communication between teacher and student, he is in fact teaching the student to view the expert role as one that excludes collaboration between client and professional. If such a professor is sufficiently unfrozen by pressures from students, colleagues, and deans, he might well

---

[3] It can, of course, be argued that it is usually the *culture* of the system that must be changed in the first place, but when we make that kind of statement we usually mean that only some key elements of the culture need to be changed. Those elements, when changed, must still be congruent with the remainder of the culture.

imitate a colleague and try a more collaborative teaching model. But if the assumptions underlying that model run counter to the norms of autonomy which the professor continues to hold, he will either misuse the collaborative model or abandon it after a few trials. The important point to recognize is that such an outcome does not mean that the model was wrong, but only that it was incongruent with the culture of the particular system within which it was attempted.

In summary, identification or imitation is the easy way to produce change, but it runs the risk of introducing changes that will not survive. Scanning for new information and integrating such information into a solution that fits the particular system is slower and more costly but is more likely to produce innovations that will survive.

Stage 3: Refreezing Refreezing involves two basically different but equally important components. Whatever new response is attempted, it must fit into the total personality of the individual attempting it, and it must fit sufficiently into the culture of which that person is a member to be confirmed and reinforced by others. In other words, it is very difficult for an individual to sustain a change which does not fit other parts of him, and it is equally difficult to sustain a change which may fit his personality but which is incongruent with what others in his reference group or relevant social system expect of him or are willing to tolerate.

We can cite an example of these two processes from efforts to introduce a more experiential type of organizational psychology course into a traditional lecture-oriented management school. Early efforts to teach the course with a number of exercises, case discussions, and student-managed discussion sections were of uneven quality in direct proportion to the personalities and teaching styles of the professors teaching the course in any given year. If a professor who believed in experientially based learning taught the course, it went well; if a more lecture-oriented professor taught the course, it either went poorly or he redesigned the course in various subtle ways to place more emphasis on those parts with which he was comfortable. In both cases the impact on students was low, hence the issue of refreezing or integrating the course into the total system of the school did not come up.

However, more recently the course has been taught for several years in a row by a team of professors highly dedicated to experiential learning and has, as a consequence, become more effective in involving students and making them active learners. This active learning style has extended into other classes that were still being taught by the lecture method. Students began to interrupt more, to ask more questions, to challenge the style of the professor, and so on. As a consequence, the professors in these more "traditional" courses began to raise questions about what was going on in the behavioral science course and to put subtle pressure on the behavioral science professors teaching the experientially based course to ease off on what they were doing. In other words, the total culture of the school was clearly not congruent with an active-learner model. Even though the new style of teaching was refrozen in those professors who were teaching the course, their teaching behavior was not receiving confirmation from many other professors, hence the innovation did not become integrated into the total system of the school. The survival of the method will now hinge on the strength of the subculture within which the innovative professors are working. It remains to be seen whether in the future some of the norms of the school will change toward legitimating this type of course or whether the traditional cultural forces will assert themselves, creating pressures to drive out the innovation and, possibly, the people associated with it. It is also possible that ways will be found to combine elements of the innovation with traditional elements.

Similar examples may be cited from efforts to introduce sensitivity training into schools of architecture or law, efforts to introduce videotape feedback to teachers, efforts to introduce computer-aided instruction, efforts to create interdisciplinary courses, etc. Even in schools of management or business, where the teaching of business policy *requires* an interdisciplinary perspective, it has been almost impossible to get teams of professors to put together effective interdisciplinary curricula.[4]

The problem of refreezing is usually slighted in published reports of innovative activities. Once a school tries something new, it is quick to announce the innovation before it is really possible to determine whether the innovation fits into the culture of the school

[4] The policy course usually ends up in the hands of a person who has been a businessman and can therefore bring a broad perspective based on his own experience, but there is little carry-over from the policy perspectives of faculty member A to faculty member B, who may have had a different kind of practical experience.

and in what manner it will survive, if at all. This type of unstable innovation is especially likely where people are operating on the model of an experimental cell somewhere in the system, with the assumption that if the cell survives it will automatically diffuse into the rest of the system. It is equally possible that the cell will survive only as long as it bothers no one. We can cite many examples of highly innovative programs that have survived on a very small scale within a system whose values are largely incongruent with those of the experimental cell. The innovation survives because of the fund-raising skills of its proponents or because of a benign administration that chooses to support innovation, often for the (wrong) reason that it can then claim that the *total* system is innovative.

The change agent who is genuinely concerned about effective refreezing, who wants long-run stable change as his product, must concern himself with the integration of new educational ventures into the total system of the school. Even if it is logical to start with an experimental cell because this poses the least threat initially, he cannot leave the matter there and hope for spontaneous diffusion. The matter of then integrating the cell must be actively managed, and often this will take more effort than launching the experiment in the first place.

In this chapter we have described a general change model that helps identify some of the particular problems and pitfalls of any effort at planned change. In particular, it emphasizes that one cannot induce change if there is no motivation to change and one cannot induce motivation to change simply by putting more and more pressure on a person or school. Simultaneous with the pressure, there must be sufficient psychological safety to permit people to feel less threatened and less defeated by the prospects of change.

Secondly, we pointed out that change itself can occur rapidly and easily if one adopts innovations that have been tried elsewhere, or it can be slower and more costly if one invents one's *own* solutions. The advantage of the latter approach is that the changes made are more likely to be congruent with other parts of the culture of the system and hence are more likely to survive.

Finally, we pointed out that a change effort is not successfully concluded until the new beliefs, attitudes, values, or behavior patterns are integrated both into the personalities of participants and into the culture of the system that is undergoing change. Both kinds of integration are especially difficult when dealing with the academic profession because of the strong commitment in that profession to the norm of autonomy, which, in practice, means that every professor wants to remain totally in control of what happens in his own classroom. Hence he is little disposed to reinforce the innovations of his colleagues unless they happen to fit into his own style.

Given this overall model, how can we then proceed to make a more concrete diagnosis of the forces that must be managed if professional schools are to begin to change toward some of the goals we have mentioned? For this purpose we need a more concrete problem-solving model and a diagnostic approach that will be described in the next chapter.

9. Change Goals, Points of Entry, and First Steps

A program of *planned change* is typically slow and difficult. It requires careful thinking through of what the goals are, where in the system to begin to work toward those goals, and what initial steps to take in moving toward the goals. Each of these segments of the planned change process in turn requires further diagnosis and action planning.

FORCE-FIELD ANALYSIS We pointed out in the previous chapter that for any change process to begin, there must be some unfreezing on the part of the change target. If the change agent is lucky, the system to be changed is already unfrozen and ready to seek new information. In the more typical case, the individual or the system to be changed does not recognize its own need to change, has ignored, misinterpreted, or denied potentially disconfirming information, and is disposed to react defensively to any new information. In this case, it falls to the change agent to diagnose the sources of resistance, to select some of these sources as the ones to analyze and work on, and, in that process, to commit himself to certain points of entry and initial change steps.

A useful diagnostic tool for identifying and analyzing the forces acting on a system with respect to any given change target is force-field analysis (Lewin, 1947). Let us assume that one of the major change targets is to make the graduates of a given architecture school more collaborative in their orientation both toward clients and toward other professionals. We can then postulate an initial low state of collaborativeness—the vertical line in Figure 2—and ask what forces (called "driving forces") are pushing architects toward more collaborativeness and what forces (called "restraining forces") are restraining the level of collaborativeness to remain at the present low level. The important point in drawing the force field is to recognize that any given present state is the result of *many* driving and restraining forces and that the change agent has a choice concerning which of these forces he will concentrate on in trying to move the level toward more collaborativeness. Let us examine what some of these forces might be (see Figure 2).

FIGURE 2 *A force-field analysis of a given state of collaborativeness toward clients and other professionals*

Driving forces toward more collaboration	Present low level of collaborativeness	Restraining forces
A. Forces within the student		
—New values and assumptions that clients have a right to influence their environment		—Attachment to traditional heroic models that emphasize individual creativity
—Recognition of own lack of empathy for many classes of clients		—Impatience with low technical skills of clients or other professionals
—Recognition of complexity of problems and need to rely on other experts		—Own needs for prominence and recognition
—Lack of confidence in own ability to solve problems		—Emotional resistance or tension around the concept of sharing or collaboration (may be connected with why student entered a field like architecture, which is perceived as individualistic)
—Need to identify with new class of heroes (advocacy architects)		
B. Forces within the school		
—Presence of some faculty who provide a collaborative role model in their own work		—Presence of some faculty who set an individualistic role model in their own work
—Research or other funds for the development of collaborative models		—Classroom practices that emphasize one-way communication from faculty experts to student nonexperts
—Workshops, seminars, T-groups, etc., that train students directly in the skills of working with others		—Scholarly and research traditions that emphasize individual work and recognition
—Project teams that require several students to work with each other		—Traditions within the profession that are communicated via alumni, written materials, faculty, and visitors
C. Forces within the profession		
—Availability of career paths that emphasize collaborative roles		—Availability of career paths that reward and emphasize individualistic, creative performance

Before we comment on and explain some of the forces shown in Figure 2, we should reemphasize why we drew such a diagram in the first place. Its prime purpose is to force the change agent and members of the system to be changed to identify and analyze *all* the forces that are acting on a given system and to avoid the temptation to limit their thinking to one or two forces even though they may be quite relevant. The most relevant forces are often the ones most difficult to do anything about. If the change agent limits himself to working on those forces that initially occur to him, he may well embark on a program that will fail.

This trap operates especially in regard to the choice of whether to work on driving forces or restraining forces. In most change situations, once one has identified a change goal like "more collaborativeness," one tends immediately to think of the driving forces that will aid movement toward the target. Thus, in the case shown in Figure 2, one might immediately think of inserting workshops or training programs that emphasize more collaboration. However, if one ignores the restraining forces, one is risking the possibility that they are powerful enough to offset whatever positive effects the workshop or training program may have. For example, if there are no new career lines available, if there are no faculty or other role models of collaborative work, if the reward system is clearly biased toward individual effort, then adding driving forces will simply not work. At best it will be a waste of time; at worst it will increase the total tension of the system by stimulating increased resistance to something that may be perceived as threatening. On the other hand, if one can identify significant restraining forces and allocate one's effort toward reducing their effect, then the system often moves almost by itself in the desired direction because there are usually already enough driving forces acting on it.

How would this strategy of change apply to the diagram we have shown? First of all, one would want to go down the *right* side and assess the actual strength of the various restraining forces. For example, the selection system of many schools of architecture may be strongly biased toward admitting only those students whose pattern of needs and motives is strongly individualistic and narcissistic. If this is the case, obviously it would be well to change the admissions system before one inserted new curriculum packages that emphasize collaboration. Similarly, if one finds that collaborative models are threatening either to faculty or students (as has been the case with the introduction of T-groups into architecture departments in at least three major schools), it becomes imperative to work out supportive mechanisms that reduce the threat. Such mechanisms were not worked out in any of the three schools; consequently the T-groups were dropped with the rationalization that they were not relevant to the curriculum (even though some faculty and many students continued to want them).

Moving down the list of restraining forces, the change agent should assess the degree to which the faculty style, the manner of conducting classes, the way in which the jury system works on student projects, the kinds of projects that are assigned and the manner in which they are graded, etc., support an individualistic style of working. If the teaching-learning system of the school itself sets a strong role model of individualistic work, it is unlikely that special programs emphasizing the collaborative work will ever get off the ground or be able to sustain themselves. Similarly, if there are no jobs or career lines for graduates who take a more collaborative role model of architecture as their own preferred style, it is pointless to train such graduates.

Having systematically examined the list of restraining forces, the next step for the change agent is to identify those restraining forces that are of sufficient potency that they can be assumed to be *real barriers* to the desired change. For each of the forces thus identified as barriers, the diagnostic process can and should be repeated in order to get a better understanding of the nature of the barrier. Let us illustrate by assuming that one key barrier is the present system of teaching and the manner in which student performance is assessed. One can again set up a force field, taking as the present level the degree to which the system rewards individual behavior (see Figure 3).

Among the driving forces are strong demands from many students to be more involved in decision making pertaining to their curriculum as well as pressure from some faculty members who feel that students should be more involved. Furthermore, the nature of projects that students work on is becoming more complex and requires team effort. On the restraining side, however, are some students and many faculty who believe strongly that total control of the curriculum and the teaching process should continue to reside in the faculty who are, by training, the experts in those areas. These beliefs are bolstered by strong academic traditions that learning is a highly individual process and that therefore all evaluation of student performance should be made individually, which,

FIGURE 3 *Force-field analysis of why teaching-learning system of a school is typically individually oriented*

Driving forces toward a collaborative system	Present level of emphasis on individualism	Restraining forces
A. Forces within the student		
—Desire to be more involved in determining own curriculum and methods of evaluation	→	—Dependence feelings and resistance to taking on responsibility
—Fear of arbitrary control by faculty	→	—Habits of passivity built up through previous educational experiences
—New career concepts that involve new roles and new combinations of knowledge and skills	→	—Feelings of having nothing to contribute; actual lack of expertise relevant to the problem
	←	—Lack of motivation to put in the extra work required in a collaborative model
B. Forces within the school		
—Faculty desire to get better feedback on their own teaching	→	—Emotional resistance to being evaluated by students
—Pressure from administrators to obtain information for purposes of evaluating teaching performance	→	—Model of the faculty member as a professional who evaluates his own performance or subjects it only to peer evaluation
—Administrative pressure to give students more power to reduce disruption and revolts	→	—Prior history of unsuccessful attempts to involve students
—Student projects that require collaboration		—Belief that students do not know what is best for them, hence should not have a voice in curriculum content or teaching style
	→	—Belief that learning is individual and should be individually evaluated
	←	—Fear that power sharing or collaboration will lead to anarchy or total abdication by faculty
	←	—Lack of personal experience in collaborative situations
	←	—Record keeping and grading systems organized around individual performance
C. Forces within the profession	←	—Job placement puts emphasis on individual, not collaborative, skills in terms of what employers ask for on recommendations
—Scope of projects that require collaborative skills	→	

in turn requires individual performance on projects and tests. Most professors also confuse collaboration with abdication. Having been brought up in a system in which they were trained to be the autonomous decision maker, they strongly fear that sharing certain kinds of decisions with students will lead to anarchy and *complete* loss of control of the curriculum by the faculty. Another restraining force is that most faculty members themselves don't know how to work in team situations and don't know how to evaluate the performance of others if that performance is part of a collaborative effort. I have observed this in my own teaching, in which I will go so far as to let two students do a joint thesis project but then will encourage individual written products because that is the only thing I know how to evaluate.

The whole paraphernalia of record keeping and accounting acts as a restraining force in social systems. Registration materials, credits, grades, letters of recommendation, and other items of information about students are always coded in such a way that giving joint evaluations to project teams or giving group grades is administratively difficult if not impossible. Consequently, for a given faculty member to stimulate collaborative work among student teams, he must surmount a whole series of administrative hurdles. Some of the most dramatic educational change programs I know of became possible only when an agreement was made with the university administration to give block credit for an entire semester or year to all students registered in the experimental program and for the program to take over all other administrative matters such as grading and record keeping.

A final and most important restraining force against more collaborative work in professional schools is that the professions themselves have not yet learned to value collaborative skills, hence do not ask for assessment of such skills when they request letters of recommendation for graduates. If architectural firms made it a regular practice to ask the architecture department to evaluate its graduates on their ability to work on a team with lawyers and economists, this would have a strong unfreezing effect on the departments and would stimulate more experiments with collaborative methods.

As one reviews these sets of forces, it becomes clear why educational change is difficult and time-consuming. But the method of systematically reviewing driving and restraining forces, identifying key barriers, and further diagnosing what forces are acting on those barriers makes it possible to develop a systematic change program that has some chance of unfreezing, changing, and refreezing the existing system. Once this general plan has emerged (in terms of which forces are to be manipulated), the next step is to devise a concrete action plan in terms of some point of entry or intervention into the present educational system.

The point of entry into the system (the person or persons with whom the change agent begins to work) will be determined primarily by diagnosis of the barriers to the change goal and secondarily by a set of further criteria which interrelate and which help identify the feasibility or potency of whatever intervention is to be made. For example, one may identify faculty attitudes as the prime barrier to more collaborative faculty-student activities, suggesting that the faculty must somehow be involved in the change process, but one may wish to start that process at the level of the academic administration, senior faculty, junior faculty, students, special faculty in special disciplines, outside funding agencies, etc. The change agent then needs a further set of criteria to help in the selection of the specific entry point. Five such criteria can be identified:

1 Degree of access to the entry person or system

2 Linkage of the entry person or system to other parts of the system

3 Suitability of the change goal for the entry system under consideration

4 Leverage of the change agent on the entry system

5 Vulnerability of the entry system to being changed in the desired direction

Let us briefly examine each of these criteria.

1 *Access* It goes without saying that if the change agent does not have access to a given person or system, he cannot consider that person or system as an initial change target. Obvious as this point seems, it nevertheless needs to be discussed because many change programs make glib assumptions about "starting at the top of the organization" or "raising enough money to support a new program" or "getting old Prof. So and So involved" without ever considering seriously how good their access is to the top, or to the foundation that will give the money, or to old Prof. So and So. If the change agent decided, for example, that he must get the president of the university involved if the change program in a professional school is to be successful, he may well spend the first six months or so of his program gaining that access. On the other hand, if access is that difficult, the change agent may develop an entirely different strategy that is not based on that particular entry system. In any case, access must be explicitly considered in developing a change program.

2 *Linkage* Linkage refers to the degree to which the entry system is connected to other parts of the total system such that if a change is produced in it, that change will be diffused to other parts of the system. The usual argument for starting a change program at the top of a power hierarchy

rests on the assumption that if the powerful members of the system change, they will then induce similar changes in other parts of the system; they have high linkage. In the typical industrial organization this logic leads to working with key executives at the top of the organization (if one has access to them); in the typical academic institution the power is more evenly divided between faculty and administration and is more diffused by departments or disciplinary groups. Consequently, in diagnosing the linkage of a potential entry point, one must be careful not to assume that the dean has the best linkage; often certain professors have better linkage than members of the administration.

One of the key problems of initiating change in an experimental unit of a larger school system is that the change may be very suitable for that unit, but the linkage of the unit to the rest of the school system is so low that no effective diffusion takes place. For example, in one large university there is an experimental education unit that has built up a staff of very creative educational innovators, but none of them have formal faculty status. The work of this unit has relatively little impact on the rest of the university, as it is viewed by most of the regular faculty as "soft-headed," "idealistic," and as dealing only with "special student populations."

3 *Suitability* Suitability refers to the degree of fit between the goals of the first intervention or action steps and what would be an appropriate change for the entry system being considered. A particular change goal may be unsuitable because of the personality of the individual being considered as an entry point, or because of his position, or because of a variety of other factors. For example, the initial intervention might be to try a collaborative curriculum-planning experiment between a key faculty member and a group of students. However, that faculty member may be teaching a highly convergent basic science course for which collaboration is minimally suitable. On the other hand such a joint planning team might be very suitable for a practicum course or a course in the behavioral sciences. The change agent must then weigh the costs and benefits of a more suitable intervention with a less well-linked professor or a less suitable intervention with a better-linked professor.

4 *Leverage* The ideal change target by the first three criteria might nevertheless *not* be practical because the change agent has no leverage on that person. In other words, he may have planned a great intervention, may have identified the person or persons who should initiate this change because of their linkage, accessibility, and the suitability of the change goal for them, but if the change agent has no means of influencing them, he must select some other entry system. In universities this is a common problem because, by their background and training, professors tend to be a relatively uninfluenceable group. The norms of autonomy insulate them from influence attempts. Such uninfluenceability operates particularly with respect to internal change agents and with respect to change agents who

are perceived as knowing little about the particular discipline which the professor is teaching. If internal leverage is too low because of either of these factors, the change agent may have to go outside the system and stimulate change through raising some research or development funds that can only be used for certain classes of educational innovations. Or, the change agent may attempt to locate someone influential in the particular professor's discipline and work through that person. For example, I have seen a case in which an intervention suggested to a mathematician by a psychologist was rejected out of hand, but the identical intervention suggested by another mathematician was accepted without question.

5   *Vulnerability*   Often the change agent has access to an entry system that is well linked, for which the change would be suitable, and in which he has some leverage, but he nevertheless decides not to proceed because he concludes that the entry system is not sufficiently unfrozen *to be able to make the change that is called for.* For example, the change agent may have available new curriculum materials that stimulate a different kind of teacher-student interaction but may decide not to push those materials even to a seemingly willing audience because of an assessment that the faculty member's attitudes are so set in a traditional mold that he would not be able to use interactive materials. Many programs of performance appraisal and management in industry such as "management by objectives" have failed because they were introduced to a group of managers whose underlying attitudes were incongruent with the superior-subordinate collaboration called for in the new program. The same kind of phenomenon will occur with collaborative teaching packages unless the change agent first develops a program of changing faculty attitudes and assumptions about the teaching-learning process.

Ultimately, the change agent must check possible entry systems against all these criteria and then decide which entry system will provide the best chances for a change to be successfully initiated, diffused to other parts of the system, and refrozen so that it becomes a durable part of the regular system of the school. Such an exercise can be demanding and time-consuming when there are a number of alternative entry systems to consider, but it is better to spend time and effort in careful preliminary planning than to make a change attempt that has a high risk of failure and a consequent high risk of discrediting the change agent.

FIRST STEPS   Studies of the change process consistently come up with one key finding: if change is to be accepted and to become part of the regular system, the parties to be changed must be involved *early* in the *diagnostic* and change *planning* process. In other words, once an entry system has been selected, the first step most likely to succeed is to *involve the entry system in some of the same diagnostic procedures that the change agent has already gone through* rather than confronting the entry system with a proposal or recommendation. Such involvement has two advantages: (1) it provides a check on whether the change agent has analyzed the driving and restraining forces accurately; and (2) it involves the change *target* (initially the entry system) in the process of managing the change effort, thus ensuring a better understanding of whatever new program is developed and ensuring reliable implementation because it is now *their* program rather than something imposed from the outside.

For example, the change agent may have as his goal the implementation of better feedback from students to faculty on the content and style of teaching. One common model that *ignores* most of the above considerations is to develop a technically sound questionnaire and convince the dean of the school and president of the student body to use the questionnaire in all courses taught in that school. This model typically ignores possible sources of resistance and possible alternative points of entry. The result in at least two cases I know of is that the faculty make relatively little time available during class for filling out the questionnaire, communicate to students their own lack of commitment to the method, and, as a result, get very low response rates from students (whose rationalization is that there is little point in spending much time on a questionnaire that "no one will pay attention to anyway").

A model more congruent with the change strategies outlined in this book would be to go to individual faculty members who are well linked, accessible, vulnerable to change, and influenceable, with the general goal of increasing student-faculty feedback. If one or more such faculty can be located, the change agent should then bring them together with one or more interested students to explore how to devise a system for improving student-to-faculty feedback. Such a group should jointly do some version of a force-field analysis to explore the various possible barriers to feedback and develop a solution that makes sense *to them* given those barriers. Once they have a system in operation, other interested faculty should be involved in a similar diagnostic exercise with the solution of the first group being considered as *only one alternative* solution. Successive groups may come up with different systems of getting feedback from students, but in each case the systems will be one that they have helped to invent and will therefore use more effectively.

This discussion can now be related back to our earlier point about *identification* (imitation) versus *scanning* as a change strategy. Looking at what others are doing can be a valuable source of ideas for one's own class or school, but the risk is so high that it will not fit and therefore not be refrozen that it is incumbent on the change agent to stimulate as much as he can a scanning approach and the development, from a variety of other models, of a solution that a given faculty member or school can really see as suitable to *their own needs.* To ensure the suitability of the solution, they must go through some of the same diagnostic steps that the change agent went through in selecting his targets and his points of entry. If this process is short-circuited, the risk is high of initial rejection or mere lip service to innovations that will then not be refrozen and hence are a waste of time for all parties concerned.

In Chapter 8 we outlined a general change model that draws attention to the importance of first unfreezing a system and then inducing change by a strategy that will maximize the probability that changes made will be refrozen both at the individual and at the system level. In this chapter we focused on what the change agent can actually do to diagnose the state of a system by a sequence of force-field analysis, identification of key barriers, further force-field analyses on key barriers, and, finally, selection of a particular force or forces that he will attempt to change. These become the immediate change goals and require the further specification of a point of entry, a place to start a change effort. We identified five criteria—access, linkage, suitability, leverage, and vulnerability—for deciding the appropriateness of a given point of entry. Finally, we argued that the correct first step in almost any change effort is the involvement of the change target or entry system in the diagnostic process itself to ensure that the change programs selected will fit the needs of the change target and will, therefore, be refrozen.

10. *Innovative Mechanisms for Professional Education*

Most of the barriers that we have identified in the preceding chapters reflect (1) the attitudes and perspective of faculty members and/or practicing professionals; (2) the structural rigidities of academic administrative procedures, calendars, curricula, and physical plants; and (3) the structural rigidities of early career paths and occupational socialization practices. Given these barriers, a realistic way to bring about educational change is to. find some educational innovations which can be fitted into or around the present system, innovations which will gradually encourage the kinds of flexibilities for which we have argued but which will not immediately threaten the basic structure of the school and the profession. Examples of such innovations may be found in the new kinds of undergraduate programs that have sprung up in new colleges and within more established institutions. Such new programs utilize educational formats or mechanisms which are just as applicable to professional education but which have not yet been tried out systematically.[1]

Many of the mechanisms we will discuss below have been proposed as *the* answer to whatever is said to ail the educational establishment. We wish to forewarn the reader that our own view is that these mechanisms will ultimately be of use only when used *in combination with each other* in an integrated format. The educational change agent may well begin with just one of these mechanisms, but if he stops when one of them has been accepted, he is

[1] An excellent review of *broad* categories of innovation applicable to professional education may be found in Lewis Mayhew's review for the Carnegie Commission (1970) and his subsequent more detailed analysis (in press). The major difference between his review and our own analysis is that we are giving more detail and are focusing more on the *process* of creating change.

not really helping the school move toward the kinds of flexibilities we have identified as important.[2]

We also wish to forewarn the reader that we are not attempting here a review of all the varieties of educational innovations that have occurred in the last several decades. Instead, we have selected a set of such innovations and described them at their best, usually by giving an example or a case of how they have been used in a highly convergent disciplinary area. Unfortunately these mechanisms have acquired labels that have come to connote a whole range of educational activities. We wish to caution the reader that we are using the labels in a rather specific sense to apply to the particular models we will present.

As a final caution we should note that the various mechanisms overlap with each other in varying degrees. Each mechanism highlights some aspect of the complex relationship between teacher, student, and curriculum content, but most of the mechanisms can and do blend into each other. We will discuss two sets of mechanisms, one applying primarily to the professional school, itself, and one applying primarily to the early career of the professional.

A. *Mechanisms applicable to formal professional education*
  1. *Self-paced study*
  2. *Independent study*
  3. *Concentrated study*
  4. *Small-group and seminar-tutorial methods*
  5. *Project- or problem-centered study*
  6. *Practicum or clinical experience*
  7. *Work-study programs, off-campus study, co-op programs and internships*

B. *Mechanisms applicable to the early career*
  1. *Apprenticeships*
  2. *Career halfway houses, interdisciplinary service centers*
  3. *Workshops and other concentrated postgraduate educational activities*

[2] An excellent example of such "monomania" has been the attitude toward innovations based on new technology such as films, videotapes, or the computer. Whichever bit of technology is being touted, it is touted typically as the entire answer to all our problems. Yet it is clear that computers, films, etc., will only reach their full utility when combined carefully with other educational elements in a new and coherent kind of program.

The reader will note from scanning this list that many of the labels apply to mechanisms presently in use in professional education and socialization. In those cases, we will be trying to highlight innovative uses of traditional mechanisms.

Self-paced study

The concept of self-paced study derives from a learning model that assumes that learning takes place only if the student makes some *active* response to whatever material is presented to him and if the response leads to some *consequence:* better understanding, the solution to a problem, a passing grade, etc. (Keller, 1968). Further, the notion of self-pacing assumes that individuals learn at different rates and that therefore it makes no sense to require a large group of students (as in the typical lecture-recitation course) to cover the same material at some "average" pace and to be prepared, at a given time, to benefit from a lecture. In practice, this usually means that students in a self-paced course are released from the requirement to attend regularly scheduled lectures and to complete homework assignments according to some fixed schedule. Most programmed instruction, whether computer-aided or simply printed in a programmed textbook, is built on these assumptions. It puts the learner in control of the pacing of his learning and gives him frequent, reliable feedback on how he is doing. The notion of self-pacing as we are using it implies that the material to be learned can be broken down into components or units that are in some way cumulative.

The application of this system that is most relevant to professional education is the self-paced elementary physics course taught at MIT (Green, 1969) as one option to taking physics (the other option is basically a lecture-recitation format). The course consists of (1) a number of prepackaged, self-contained units of material that were designed by the faculty; (2) a study guide that makes explicit the concepts to be mastered and suggests a study method for approaching the unit, including readings, possible experiments, or a taped lecture; (3) a professor who functions as the administrator of the course and who gives occasional lectures on key concepts; (4) a set of tutors who are students roughly two to three years ahead of those taking the course; and (5) a set of examinations on each unit.

Any number of students can take the course. A student starts with a unit obtained from the administrative headquarters room of the course. He works on the unit until he feels he has mastered it and then asks for an examination on that unit. Examinations are always given on the day of the week when the tutors and the professor are available for consultation. After the student has completed the examination, he takes it to one of the tutors who grades it and then discusses all the answers with the student. They jointly decide whether the student has mastered that unit or not. If he has mastered it, he goes on to the next unit; if he has not, he repeats the unit. The professor is on call for consultation if the decision is ambiguous. The tutorial sessions with the senior students can be as long or as short as either student or tutor desires. The final grade in the course is based on performance in the regular midterm and final examinations given in the more traditionally taught version of that physics course.

At Georgetown University, an introductory psychology course is built on a similar model (Ferster, 1968). The syllabus is divided into sections, each section containing a set of readings taken either from the text or from journals or other outside sources. The essential characteristic of this program is the use of interviews to provide feedback and to help the student evaluate his own progress. When a student feels he has covered a section of the syllabus, he schedules an interview, during which he discusses what he has learned with another student in the course. The listener gives positive and negative feedback; then together they decide whether the learner has mastered the material. If the interview is successful, the student goes on to the next section. If it is not, he reviews the material and schedules another interview. At the end of three to five sections, he takes a short written exam to demonstrate mastery. There is no penalty for failure to "pass" any interview or exam. The final grade is determined by how much of the syllabus the student has covered.

A self-paced course at North Carolina Central University, called *Photography for Teachers,* is organized into 10 learning activity packages (LAP's), each of which contains (1) a statement of purpose for the unit; (2) a list of learning objectives which specifies exactly what is expected of the student upon completion of the package; (3) a pretest, which is self-administered and meant to help the student assess his needs with respect to the particular LAP objectives; (4) a list of learning-activity alternatives from which the student can choose activities which most nearly match his own preferred learning style (readings, recorded lectures, films, the teacher, etc.); (5) a post test, also self-administered, through which the student can evaluate his own progress; and (6) instructions regarding teacher evaluation. When a student has completed a LAP and feels satisfied that he has met its objectives, he goes to the teacher for evaluation, giving him either a written or manual demonstration of mastery. He either passes the evaluation or is encouraged to work more on the unit and repeat the test. There are no formal classes unless students petition for one (Flaum, 1970).

It should be noted that these self-paced models not only allow the student to cover the material at his own rate but also clearly set teacher performance expectations and provide continual feedback to the student without the usual negative pressure of exams (since there is no penalty for "failing" a test or evaluation). Thus the tutors and the professor function in a consultative role, as resources and aides, rather than in an authoritarian role, as evaluators and as the prime sources of knowledge. The student is thus more able to expose his uncertainties to them, can demand more of their time, and can use them as role models.

Even though this model of self-paced study allows maximum flexibility for the student in pacing himself throughout the semester, it fits easily into the normal academic calendar by linking itself to regular examinations and a fixed termination point. Thus it may be introduced with minimal disturbance to the rest of the educational system. It has been introduced at MIT in a number of courses and has been limited only by the ability of the faculty members to develop the requisite course materials. It is usually introduced as an alternative to the traditional lecture-recitation-based method of taking a given course, allowing for the fact that many students prefer the more traditional course method.[3]

The major limitation of self-paced study is that it lends itself easily only to certain kinds of material. It is clearly most relevant to convergent bodies of knowledge that can be translated into

---

[3] Self-paced courses, such as the MIT model and others referred to, are not suitable to the learning style of every student. It is not an unstructured program and does not give the student the freedom to decide what his own goals are or what he will learn. Some students in the MIT program complained that it was more highly structured than a traditional course (Green, 1969), particularly since the designers of the course laid out in the study guide exactly what they felt the most appropriate study method for each unit would be.

learning units, for which objective tests can be designed, and in which mastery can fairly easily be measured by written tests. Most professional schools have, as part of their basic science core, material that probably could be converted into units suitable for self-paced study. If such courses were introduced, students could more easily plan a flexible curriculum for themselves and get involved in projects that might require some time away from campus. It would free much of the faculty to offer elective courses and to help students with student-initiated projects.

Independent study

Independent study and self-paced study are often confused because they both involve the underlying assumption that the student will learn more if he is given the freedom to manage his own learning to a certain degree. But they are entirely different in the degree to which they are linked to a given set of curriculum materials. While self-paced study is generally linked to a set of curriculum units designed by the faculty, independent study implies a vastly greater degree of freedom for the student, ranging from the design of a single course to the design of an entire undergraduate program. The independent study *may* involve attending regular classes but packaging sets of courses into a new kind of program of study, or it may involve a different form of study — projects, work-study periods, teamwork with other students, etc.

The essence of the independent study idea is to create a situation in which the student can make a joint decision with one or more faculty members about some learning goals to be achieved, some means to achieve them, and some criteria by which to determine whether or not they have been achieved. But the student is freed from traditional curricula, course sequences, requirements, prerequisites, etc., except insofar as he and his faculty advisers decide to keep any of these formal elements in the student's program. Even more important, the student can be freed from residence requirements, making it possible for him to study part-time and to study where his family or job are rather than where his campus is. Some systems of independent study formalize the procedure to the extent of negotiating a "learning contract," an agreement entered into by the student and some faculty members who function as advisers, tutors, and possibly, though not necessarily, as evaluators of the outcome. The agreement covers the general area of study, depth of coverage, and output criteria to be used in evaluation. The contract may specify some external evaluation criterion or an evaluation committee that may have on it other students, faculty, and professionals.

Some independent study programs function primarily within the university. For two examples of such programs, we can cite MIT's Unified Science Studies Program (USSP; Morgan, 1970) and Experimental Study Group (ESG; Valley, 1971). Both are options available to approximately 50 freshman and 50 sophomores as replacements for the regular sequence of required science and humanities courses, and both grant block credit for an entire semester of work without specific consideration of what the student worked on. Students and faculty can thus jointly plan one or more years of work without being tied to a course structure.

The USSP program is based primarily on projects, some of which are developed by students themselves and some of which are based on staff-developed units of material that suggest experiments, projects, problems, and readings. In the first year of the program, some students chose to make use of this prepared material, but most chose projects of their own (including such topics as "Territoriality in Rodents: Rat Control Using High Frequency Sound"; "Housing in Guatemala: Social and Technological Considerations"; "Reducing Pollution in the Charles River"; and so on).[4] Some students did not undertake long-term projects but concentrated instead on self-directed study of regular MIT subjects by auditing lectures and reading independently. The program allowed them the flexibility to explore in depth areas of particular interest to them and to skip or minimize those areas in which they were less interested.

To help students fulfill institute requirements, there were two-week concentrated study courses available in calculus and physics during the second semester. In addition there were several seminars, held in response to student requests, on a wide variety of topics from any number of disciplines. Students who, in conjunction with their project work, felt the need of some basic science

[4] Note the interdisciplinary nature of these projects. Independent study encourages interdisciplinary work because it releases the student from discrete subjects in discrete disciplines. The new program in human biology at Stanford is an explicitly interdisciplinary degree, allowing the student maximum flexibility to put together his own package of courses from biology, sociology, law, genetics, education, psychology, etc., and to pursue such interests as the sociological implications of heart transplants or man as an adaptive animal ("New Human Biology," November 1970).

courses were encouraged to audit or take for credit any regular institute course.

Each student project had at least one faculty supervisor who worked closely with the student or students on the project. In addition, each student had an adviser to whom he was responsible for defending his course of study. In order to broaden the student's resource base, he was also asked to pick another faculty member, neither his adviser nor his project supervisor, and to present his project to him. He was asked to keep an ongoing journal of his work and to make that journal available to the entire USSP staff for inspection. At the end of each semester, students were asked to present a summary of the first term's work and, at some point, a colloquium to students and faculty, which was meant to be a vehicle for sharing knowledge and experiences with the group rather than a means of evaluation. Evaluation is handled on the basis of "pass-incomplete." In order to pass, the student must convince his adviser that he has lived up to his learning goals.

The ESG program goes even further in abandoning the project structure and substituting for it an open negotiation between students and faculty on what is to be learned, by what method, and for what length of time. ESG is essentially a learning community in which part-time faculty members, graduate tutors, advanced undergraduates, and full-time freshman come together to explore the learning process. Great emphasis is given to community meetings, small-group seminars, and planned or spontaneous tutorial sessions. The unstructured environment stimulates self-examination and facilitates the setting of realistic learning goals. For many of the students the opportunity to think through their goals for weeks or even months becomes a major source of learning, especially if they have come from a highly paced high school science curriculum. Once students discover what they really want to work on, they work more efficiently and are able to go much further into a subject in a shorter period of time. Evaluation of performance is handled, as in USSP, by a faculty adviser who examines the student by mutually agreed upon means and then certifies that a certain amount of work has been completed.

To support the learning process, ESG and USSP have their own computer consoles, videotape equipment, films, libraries, and any other learning aids which either faculty or students suggest as potentially helpful. Both programs have also used behavioral scientists to run "learning groups" focused on the dynamics of the learning process itself, especially on the interaction between emotional and cognitive factors in learning.

These programs open up for the student the entire range of university resources without tying him down to the regular curriculum. They encourage his involvement with faculty members and other students as consultants and fellow learners, without competition for grades. Involvement in these programs makes available to him not only special seminars and group meetings on topics in which he is genuinely interested but also the whole range of MIT courses if he wants them. Independent study thus allows the student maximum flexibility as to where, when, and how he learns.

Another advantage to independent study is that the student may be freed from the requirement of studying in a single university or limiting his experiences to strictly "academic" ones.[5] Perhaps the most advanced model of an interuniversity independent study program is the Union Graduate School doctoral program (*The Union Graduate School,* 1971). Students in this program are expected to do a major portion of their study outside of any formal curriculum by concentrating on independent reading and research; but they may also take courses at any university in the world, either at one of the associated schools (of which there are 18)[6] or by special arrangement anywhere else. They are encouraged to study as apprentices to distinguished leaders in their field or in some highly educative social situation such as an underdeveloped country, inner city, or planned community. The only residence requirement of this program is a four-to six-week colloquium that the student attends near the beginning of his graduate work. These colloquiums are held several times a year at each of the several union centers around the country. The purposes of the colloquium are (1) to consider the relationship of graduate education to the needs of society; (2) to develop the student's insight and self-

[5] Off-campus study, which may be considered a form of independent study, will be discussed later.

[6] The parent organization is the Union for Experimenting Colleges and Universities, including Antioch, Bard, Chicago State, Friends World, Goddard, Hofstra University, Loretto Heights, the University of Massachusetts (School of Education), the University of Minnesota, Monteith New College at Sarasota, Northeastern, Illinois State, the University of the Pacific, Roger Williams, Staten Island Community College, Stephens, Westminister, and the University of Wisconsin at Green Bay.

awareness through human relations workshops; and (3) to aid the student in making plans for his program of study. Most of the students, during this colloquium period, are expected to formulate their plans of study and to discuss them with fellow students and advisers. At this time the student also selects his own advising committee, who later serve as his evaluation committee. It must consist of himself, two or more adjunct faculty advisers, a minimum of two fellow students, and a member of the Union core faculty. The student is expected, as part of the learning contract, to communicate regularly with this group either by mail, by follow-up meetings to the colloquiums, or by visiting one of the regional centers. Small groups of students and perhaps adjunct faculty advisers are expected to meet occasionally at the centers to review plans, pursue areas of mutual interest, and stimulate the progress of individuals. After a year, the student and his committee jointly decide whether or not he has fulfilled his "contract" by developing the plans agreed upon, by responding to advice from peers and advisers, and by performing at a sufficiently high level. If the student is certified at this time, it is expected that he will complete his doctoral work. In place of the Ph.D. dissertation, the student normally completes a "project demonstrating excellence," which may take the form of traditional research, the publishing of a book, the design and implementation of a significant social change, or the creation of a substantial piece of art, music, or literature. This project is designed in cooperation with his committee to take into account his goals and abilities. The core Union faculty at Yellow Springs, Ohio, conduct the initial and any subsequent colloquiums and visit the various centers to give advice and aid. At each center there are full-time and some part-time adjunct faculty who are available at any time to visiting students. In addition there are some special adjunct faculty members who make themselves available for the duration of the work of a single student in whom they are particularly interested.

While self-paced study has a facilitating structure built into it via units, exams, and tutors, independent study is essentially a system for letting the student proceed in whatever way makes sense to him and his advisers with a minimum of common structure among students. Independent study is thus much more flexible, but it demands more of the faculty advisory structure and presumes a degree of independence and maturity of students that is frequently not there. Independent study becomes for many students an escape hatch or a great source of frustration unless a sympathetic faculty adviser helps in the establishment of a realistic learning contract and sets up a feedback system that helps the student assess his own progress toward his goals. This mechanism tends to fail in those educational systems in which the faculty is initially unsympathetic to the idea of students having a voice in setting learning objectives.[7] If they are unsympathetic, they tend to do a poor job of advising and thus create a self-fulfilling prophecy; i.e., the student will indeed do poorly if given independence.

Independent study as part of the professional curriculum — because of its flexibility and because it provides opportunities to develop new areas of inquiry, especially from an interdisciplinary point of view — should be explored far more widely than it has been. In principle, almost any kind of material can be learned in this manner except those skills and attitudes that require constant surveillance and feedback from faculty or senior learners. It only requires commitment on the part of some faculty members to spend some time advising, checking progress, and evaluating outcomes.

Concentrated study
Concentrated study is a relatively highly structured approach to learning a given body of material by concentrating all the teaching-learning effort on *only that material* for a given length of time. The idea of using concentrated study as a teaching method is based in part on the observation that most students study in concentrated form even during a normal semester. That is, they tend to concentrate on one subject at a time, almost to the exclusion of the others, particularly near midterm or end-of-term exams. A student will often spend a week or so on a given subject doing most of the reading he has not found the time to do earlier or writing a term paper he has theoretically been working on all term. Inserting

[7] Some innovative undergraduate programs consider it crucial that students have a voice in deciding curriculum issues even within a regular course structure. At Southern Illinois University, a new program called Learning through Integrated Faculty-Student Teamwork (LIFT) attempts to involve students at all levels of curriculum planning — in designing course objectives, reviewing teaching materials, scheduling classroom hours and laboratory activity, and deciding on criteria for peer evaluation. To facilitate this, the junior year for about 40 students is block-scheduled and is the responsibility of 8 faculty members in teams of 4. The block scheduling permits courses to be of any length required to cover the material decided on (Myers, K., personal communication, April 1968).

regular concentrated study courses into the curriculum allows this kind of learning to occur without making the student feel anxious about other subject work piling up around him.

A common example of concentrated study already in use in many regular curricula is the workshop or one-week seminar on a given topic. Many of the new curriculum elements that we have suggested for professional education can best be handled in this format. For example, the applied behavioral science components dealing with (1) the diagnosis of complex social systems and client-professional relationships; (2) learning how to work in and with groups; (3) the dynamics of collaborative relationships in intra- or interprofessional teams; and (4) the obtaining of self-insight and insight into the professional role can all best be taught through participative full-time workshops. This format has proved successful not only in teaching people the *skills* of communication, interpersonal relations, and leadership but also in teaching the *content* of group dynamics and leadership theory.

For example, at the University of Cincinnati, as part of a new program of fall workshops, the College of Design, Architecture, and Art ran a workshop focused on the effectiveness of a group of participants in accomplishing a specific task. The aim was to involve the whole faculty group in planning the curriculum. A consultant was available to help the group examine its communication patterns, decision-making processes, and conflict resolution within the group ("Fall Workshops," undated).

Somewhat more rare is the use of concentrated study with regular course material that would ordinarily be covered in an entire semester. In one experiment at MIT (Parlett & King, 1971), a physics professor, engineering professor, and mathematics professor decided to teach their courses in sequence rather than simultaneously, each taking one month and asking students to concentrate only on the material of that course for that month. Fifteen students were chosen for the first trial of this course. None of them was involved in other courses at the time. They agreed to meet five days a week for approximately one month. A typical day's schedule for the course began with demonstrations and experiments in the lab in the morning followed by an hour and a half of lecture and discussion, occasionally with a short film. In the afternoon, students met in pairs with a faculty member to discuss areas of special interest to them, problems with the homework, questions about the readings, and so on. The evening was free, allowing students to read and work on problems and faculty to discuss individual progress and possible modifications for individual students.[8] In the second two weeks laboratory sessions were devoted entirely to individual projects or problems undertaken by pairs of students. All evaluation was done on a pass-fail basis, which is probably facilitated, in this type of course, by the extremely close student-faculty contact.

The obvious advantage of concentrated study as a mechanism is that it can often be sandwiched into the existing calendar. One can design workshops, intensive seminars, and concentrated study courses for vacation periods such as the summer or for the period between semesters, thus reducing the need for major administrative changes in the calendar. Concentrated study thus lends itself easily to use as a supplement to other learning modes, such as independent study. We discussed the use of concentrated study in MIT USSP program as an option for students wishing to fulfill requirements. Basic science courses could be made available in concentrated form several times during the year in any independent study program or project-centered study. When students reach a point in their own work at which they feel the need for a course in physics or chemistry in order to continue, they could interrupt their project for three or four weeks and concentrate on that particular area.

One can also create a compromise solution by teaching certain courses for an entire day or half-day, permitting the interlacing of lecture, reading, discussion, exercises, laboratory projects, and any other activity. Thus a student might take anatomy on Monday, physiology on Tuesday, biochemistry on Wednesday, and so on, each week. If concentrated study is to be used in regular courses, all or most of the courses required of a given student in a given term must use it. Such coordination, in turn, requires certain faculty attitudes and flexibilities that are often lacking. It requires some redesign of course materials and the participation of faculty members who are comfortable in the more intensive interaction engendered by the daily contact with students.

Concentrated study has been used very successfully in the

---

[8] The scheduling of a concentrated study course is limited only by one's imagination in creating interesting education designs. One could start with a reading period, followed by discussion and a short quiz, with lecture and further discussion in the afternoon. The MIT program focused on lab experiments and included two field trips during the one-month period.

teaching of languages, physics, computer programming, and many other highly convergent areas. It is most applicable to those areas in which the student must make frequent overt responses and receive good feedback in order to determine whether or not he is learning the right things. It would seem less applicable to courses in which the material requires a lot of "digestion time," such as the humanities course designed to acquaint the student with broad value issues. However, we do not mean to suggest that concentrated study is inappropriate for in-depth exploration of topics or for divergent thinking. Because of the high degree of involvement and because of the small-group learning atmosphere, which we will discuss in the next section, concentrated study encourages a deeper exploration of the material.

Another crucial advantage of concentrated study or workshop formats is that they can be handled by part-time, consulting, or adjunct faculty. Many professional schools are neither willing nor able to pay for full-time behavioral scientists and professors of management, but they could afford to hire such professors on a part-time basis to run focused, concentrated courses, a pattern which is common in business school executive-development programs and in continuing education programs for professionals generally.

Small-group and seminar-tutorial methods

A key way in which concentrated study as we have described it differs from both independent study and self-paced study is in the emphasis it puts on the small-group dimension of learning.[9] In the MIT program, students and faculty are committed to staying together for the duration of the three one-month courses. This makes possible some negotiation about the content and format of the course and significantly alters traditional student-faculty and peer group relationships. The faculty members are constantly available as consultants in problem solving and for in-depth investigation of special topics of interest; and, given that competition for grades does not exist, fellow learners can act as resources to each other.

Seminars involving one faculty member with anywhere from five to twenty students and tutorial sessions which may involve

---

[9] John King, prime designer of the MIT course described, feels it is essential to keep the student number below 20, both for student-student interaction and because of the intensity he feels is required in the faculty's relationships with students.

one faculty member with anywhere from one to five students are hardly innovations, but they have, in recent years, been used in an innovative fashion with some new goals that deserve comment. Many undergraduate innovations in recent years have concentrated on the notion of clustering students in courses, for example, maintaining a group of fifteen to thirty freshmen who take four out of five of their courses together for a whole year. It has been found that these students have higher morale and get better grades than unclustered freshmen. A second model is the living-learning group, in which students eat, sleep, study, and take most of their courses together under one roof ("Living–Learning," September 1966).

Perhaps the most obvious virtue of group learning is that students simply learn better in small instructional groups than they do in large lecture-recitation courses. Two other aspects of small-group learning should be mentioned, however, because they are crucial to some of the needs of the professions that we have discussed. The first is the conscious use of small-group learning to foster divergent thinking and creative problem solving. For example, Abercrombie (1967) points out that in a group of 12 architecture students, each of whom is working on the design of a nursing home, the likely outcome will be 12 different designs. It is not enough, she argues, to evaluate individual student designs on the basis of a teacher's criteria; rather, the most useful thing for the students is to discuss each other's designs, to gain some understanding of the thinking processes and problem-solving methods behind each design, and to come up with some criteria for evaluation agreed upon by the whole group. In this way, each student has a chance to expand his own methods of problem solving and to learn to use other members of the group as a resource.

The use of the peer group as a resource also has great applicability to the continuing education of professionals. The rapid obsolescence of many professionals may well be a function of *how* their learning took place in school. If they learned to rely exclusively on faculty as resources and saw fellow students only as competitors for good grades, they may have gotten into the habit of always looking for authoritative resources. But who will those authorities be once the professional is in private practice? He can attend seminars, sponsored by the professional association, where authoritative resource people are brought in, but on a day-to-day basis the professional could keep himself intellectually alive much better if he were habituated to seeing his peers as resources.

The use of the seminar method has been generally accepted as appropriate for content areas that require active exploration by students and in which an exchange of student opinions would be useful, i.e., humanities courses, advanced theoretical courses, courses based on value issues, and so on. In the last decade or so, however, there has been an increasing exploration of the use of seminars and small-group discussion in the highly convergent basic science courses of professional curricula, either as a supplement to or replacement for the basic lecture-recitation format (Abercrombie, 1960; Lomon, 1971). For example, Abercrombie argues cogently that key concepts such as *normal* are often semantically so ambiguous that it is necessary and desirable to discuss them in a small-group setting as a way of bringing out the different meanings that different students attach to them. She gives a vivid example of a failure to diagnose a case of scurvy because the patient had answered "yes" to the medical examiner's question of whether he ate a "normal" diet. The examiner had failed to determine that *normal* to this man meant a ·diet without vegetables. Abercrombie argues that students should discuss in depth a concept like *normal* to determine what it does and should mean as part of their basic training in diagnosis, ordinarily considered a highly convergent area.

In the last several years some MIT professors have attempted a similar kind of conversion in the area of basic physics and mathematics. The basic syllabus, homework patterns, and examination schedule have remained the same, but there are no lectures and the schedule of assignments is handled much more flexibly. Seminar time is devoted to discussing basic concepts, going over difficult problems, and whatever else the students and faculty choose to do. Graduate students are available as tutors for those students who, for one or another reason, need additional help.

Another use of the small-group format is in teaching individuals how to work in groups and in collaboration with one another — focusing on such issues as goal setting, decision making, team building, and communication processes within the context of topics not specifically related to human relations. For example, a group of architecture students can be given a team problem, such as coming up with a *single* design for a nursing home. The learning goals include not only how to improve design skills but how to learn to work with others in a team setting by periodically examining the group processes involved in working on the design problem. Another example is a course in speech pathology and audiology at the Cincinnati Speech and Hearing Center (Drexler & Wegener, 1970). The students are initially divided into groups of three or four and are asked to set their own learning goals, to decide what areas they need to study after some initial contact with patients and group discussion of the experience, and to evaluate themselves and each other. The groups discovered that almost an entire semester had to be spent investigating problem solving, team building, goal setting, and conflict resolution before they could accomplish their primary tasks. If we expect professionals to be able to work in teams and in collaboration with each other, we must design more learning experiences like these.

The use of the small-group method in management education can be illustrated by the Sloan School's Undergraduate Systems Program (now called the Undergraduate Studies Program) started in 1963 by Jay Forrester. Each year, 10 to 12 juniors become a group who take 60 percent of their work in an unstructured block-credit format and all their work on a pass-fail basis. The group must learn how to develop collaborative projects with the help of a faculty adviser who functions as a consultant to the group. To develop collaborative relations has often been time-consuming and difficult for the members, but most of them feel this was one of the major benefits of the program. An evaluation based on an alumni survey showed that this group did as well as or better than the regular Sloan School graduates in terms of acceptance into graduate school and early job experience. They differed most from the regular graduates in having higher aspirations and broader perspectives which they attributed, in part, to the program (Forrester, 1964; Considine, 1969).

In recognition of the potential benefits of small-group interaction for learning, many independent study programs require students to participate in a small-group component. The Union Graduate School, described in the section on independent study, requires each student to attend a four- to six-week colloquium during which he is expected to learn something about how he functions in a group, about his own biases and the biases of other students, and how to make use of the group as a sounding board for his own goals and plans.

The use of the small group in a nonresidential program is illustrated by the management program — leading to an M.B.A. degree — at the University of South Africa. This program is built around independent correspondence study in which the student is sent lectures, study guides, and assignments to which he responds by mail (Marais, 1970). Recognizing the extreme limitation of a straight correspondence-course format, the program also requires attendance at study groups and a residential course, one week at the beginning of each year and two weeks at the end of the last two years. The study groups are comprised of 5 to 11 students and are located throughout South Africa (there are 44 in all). An attempt is made to ensure that members of a given group represent a variety of academic backgrounds, jobs, and ages.

Each study group is given tasks to complete as a group. The groups, over a three-year period, submit some 46 reports on case studies and 24 reports on a business game, plus reports on projects undertaken by the group as a whole. During the residential periods, the students have a chance to interact with each other and with the faculty. During these periods the program also includes in-depth analyses of cases, lectures, and examinations.

The seminar-tutorial or small-learning-group form of running a course is obviously more expensive than the lecture-recitation form, but this expense has to be weighed against the educational benefits derived. For example, level of comprehension and depth of understanding of concepts tends to be higher on the average in the seminar-tutorial form. If the professional's competence hinges on such comprehension, it may well be worth the investment of faculty time to teach certain basics by this method. Another advantage of the seminar-tutorial system is that it permits much closer surveillance of the progress of each student, making it possible to identify learning barriers early enough to overcome them and thereby reducing the number of students who fail the course. If the professional school invests a great deal of money and time in a selection process that brings in high-caliber students, it often makes economic sense to use teaching mechanisms that minimize dropout or flunk-out rates. Those benefits that derive from listening to well-thought-out and well-presented lectures can still be obtained by adding a live lecture series to the course or videotaping good lectures and making the tapes available to students for viewing at those times when they are ready for a lecture.

Project- or problem-centered study
In the section on independent study we discussed the MIT Unified Science Studies Program in which, although it was not required,

most students found that the most effective way to approach self-directed learning was to pick a problem or project around which to design their program of studies. The assumption behind project-centered study as the main learning method is that the student will learn concepts and skills better if they are relevant to some problem he is trying to solve or some project he is trying to complete. Since such problems or projects often involve several disciplines, this form of study often becomes interdisciplinary as well. In other words, if the student is trying to understand why certain diseases are more prevalent in city ghettos than in other regions, he must learn something about epidemiology, medicine, sociology, chemical engineering, and whatever other field turns out to be relevant.

This approach is obvious when complex problems are the subject matter of the course. The applicability to the teaching of basic science is less obvious, but it is increasingly being used there as well. For example, premed and science students at the Worcester Polytechnic Institute, instead of taking a basic science curriculum in mathematics, biology, chemistry, and physics, pick a topic at the beginning of their studies to pursue in depth (*WPI News,* 1971). The focus is on real-world problems such as reproductive physiology, marijuana, or diabetes. The students then study whatever basic science they need to pursue their topic. The assumption is that the students will learn just as much about anatomy, protein structure, endocrines, and so forth, but they will learn it better and more quickly if they can see the relevance of the basic science to the problem they are trying to solve.

The role of the faculty is twofold in this kind of learning system: (1) they design basic project units consisting of a problem definition, a set of steps for the student to undertake to begin to work on the problem, and suggested readings, experiments, exercises, and checkpoints (such units can be published and used at other schools); (2) they are resources to be drawn on to give explanations, run seminars in topics which several students want to cover, give occasional lectures on important areas or concepts, make suggestions for readings or further steps, and advise the student on the proper sequence of selecting project units. However, the basic initiative for learning resides completely with the students. They can choose their own pace, the particular sequence of problems and projects, and whether or not they work with other students in joint projects.

In the form described above, the project-centered format might or might not be suitable for professional school education. Insofar as a professional education has strong convergent elements in it, it might be disfunctional to give students as much freedom as the MIT USSP program gives freshmen. On the other hand, the professional school could design a set of problem units equivalent to a certain number of courses, giving students the freedom to choose the pace and sequence of those units, and thereby stimulating higher motivation by making the subject matter more relevant to interesting problems. Thus first-year medical students could learn anatomy and physiology in reference to particular patients whom they had had a chance to observe; architecture students could learn basic design principles in reference to designing actual homes for the local neighborhood; law students could learn areas of the law that are relevant to particular cases they are working on or studying.

The effectiveness of these techniques depends a great deal upon the assumptions the faculty makes about the learning process and how one evaluates the outcome of learning. It is clearly easier to spell out a basic science area, lecture about it, give a complete set of readings and problems, and then test for total comprehension of that area. It is only as the professor recognizes that the student may have trouble applying the concepts to practical problems or may forget the area as soon as the test is over that he begins to weigh the relative merits of the standard disciplinary approach and the project-centered approach. The major advantage of project-centered study is that it stimulates interdisciplinary thinking. It would be most appropriate, therefore, in those areas of the professional curriculum in which interdisciplinary approaches are essential.

Practicum or clinical courses

Project- or problem-centered study attempts to make basic and applied sciences more relevant to the student by permitting him to see the relationship of the knowledge base to the practical problems that are to be solved. However, the exercise is still basically a theoretical one in that the student is not typically exposed to real clients with real problems. When a course of study does put the student into the position of dealing with real clients, we usually think of this as a practicum or clinical course. The purpose is to permit the student to integrate the basic and applied knowledge he has acquired with actual professional experience in a situation in which he is "playing for keeps." In other words, if the student makes an error in a practicum course, there are some negative consequences for the client, though such courses vary in the degree to which they will expose clients to high risks. Such courses differ from apprenticeships in that the experience occurs within the context of a curriculum planned by the faculty for which academic credit is given. The student is usually evaluated jointly by the faculty and the supervisor of the facility in which the client contact occurs.

In most professional schools practicum courses are given in the second, third, or fourth years, after the student has acquired a base of knowledge, some skill, and has "learned to think like a professional." The assumption is usually made that the first-year student should not be exposed to real clients, either because he does not know enough to handle the situation properly or because he might be too threatened by the actual responsibility.[10] It is also likely that in many professions, first-year students working on actual patients or live cases (in law) would pose a threat to the client and to the local practitioner who might see the students as infringing on his practice. Thus there are strong forces operating to limit clinical work to the later years of professional education and to special settings like teaching hospitals, where "charity cases" are available.

There is considerable opinion, however, that earlier clinical work would be beneficial to the student and to the school because it would encourage more integration of the basic and applied elements of professional education. For example, Case–Western Reserve Medical School assigns to each first year medical student an entire family for whose health and welfare he is responsible during his entire four years (Zacharias, 1967). Architecture students at the University of Cincinnati, as an option to a design requirement, can work in a community design center providing assistance to residents in improving their own environment ("Architect–Com-

[10] It should also be noted that unless the student's relationship to the academic calendar can be loosened up, it will continue to be difficult to provide realistic clinical experience, since client problems often require more intensive and more long-range commitments on the part of helpers. One of the main problems in introducing clinical work in the early part of professional training is that the student is, under the present system, too heavily loaded with regular academic work to be able to commit himself in any real way to client problems.

munity Connections," undated). Princeton and MIT are also setting up neighborhood architectural planning offices to permit first year graduate students to become directly involved with real client problems in the community. Stanford Law School has established a program in which students receive academic credit for serving as court prosecutors under the supervision of members of the faculty and deputy district attorneys ("Study of Man," February 1971). The University of Wisconsin Business School has an investments course in which students are actually given large amounts of money ($40,000) to invest to teach them the "realities" of this aspect of business operations. Obviously some professional schools have found ways of letting students "play for keeps" without running inordinate risks vis-à-vis clients.

The essential aim of clinical or practicum work is to permit the student to test himself in a situation requiring real professional decisions. For this process to be educational, however, it is essential that the student receive good feedback on the consequences of his judgments and decisions. The feedback ideally comes either from another professional in the situation or from a faculty member who has observed the student during the diagnostic and decision-making process. For example, in the new program at Stanford, law students spend eight to ten hours per week researching the cases on which they are working and three hours per week in a seminar with faculty members, police officers, practicing attorneys and deputy district attorneys, discussing their cases and their progress on them. In addition, from his experience in court and in research, each student is expected to write a research paper on criminal prosecution. Evaluation is made jointly by the student's professional supervisor and the faculty member. It is not sufficient to send students into the community to try their hand at practicing their skills; it is essential that supervision and feedback be built into the process.

Schools of medicine, social work, and education have usually been able to include clinical work as part of the regular curriculum. It is somewhat rarer to find it in schools of law, engineering, architecture, and management, partly because it is more difficult to simulate the professional role and to find clients with problems of a size small enough to be serviced by students. In these latter types of schools we therefore more often find *simulations* of clinical practice—projects undertaken by students in which the outcome is judged by the faculty but in which no real stakes are involved either because the client is hypothetical or because the client is not really dependent upon the solution, should it be inadequate. Case discussions, business games, war games, and other "exercises" are useful because they create high motivation and involvement. However, some students are beginning to express dissatisfaction with this type of pseudopractical experience (e.g., the jury process in architecture) and are demanding earlier *real* clinical exposure in all professions. They are also seeking the more interdisciplinary type of exposure which many client problems demand but which traditional clinical work minimizes.

To make available more interdisciplinary and earlier clinical experience will probably require the development of new centers of client services that would be partly staffed by full-time professionals, partly by faculty, and partly by students or apprentice professionals. Two such centers will be described below in the section on career halfway houses and community service centers.

In conclusion, some new inventions which focus on the *integration* of basic science, applied skills training, and practical experience and which permit an interdisciplinary focus on client problems are essential if clinical practicum work is to become more innovative and effective. As long as professional schools see the curriculum as a series of sequential steps from science to application to clinical work, there is little hope of making the clinical work a more relevant and effective learning experience.

Work-study programs, off-campus study, co-op programs, and internships

One step beyond clinical work or a practicum course is the insertion of periods of full-time work or study on or off campus into a total program of study. There are several versions of these kinds of programs. A *work-study* program, in essence, provides the flexibility for the student to leave his studies for a period of time either to broaden his experience or to earn enough money to keep going. If this type of program is to be successful, the curriculum must be designed in such a way that a student can leave and reenter without substantially sacrificing his educational goals.[11] In a typical work-study program, there is no necessary connection

---

[11] In Chapter 11 we will discuss the concept of modular construction of curriculum units with multiple entry points, which would provide this flexibility in professional education.

between the content of the work experience and the student's program of study.

Off-campus study, on the other hand, implies that the student's experiences away from the campus are educationally enriching, although not necessarily academically oriented, and that he receives some form of academic credit for them. One such program has been developed by the Union for Experimenting Colleges and Universities at Antioch College, Yellow Springs, Ohio (*Field Study Centers Bulletin, 1970–71*). This program, available to students at any college or university in the country, allows the student to participate in the work of service agencies at different field study centers. The student pays full tuition to his university and is enrolled there during the time he spends at the field center. He and his supervisor at the center, in cooperation with his school, determine an evaluation of the student's experience and how to allocate credit. In most instances, the student attends no formal classes while at the center; his experience is oriented toward the work he is doing in the community and what he can learn from it. He may be involved in problems relating to any number of different disciplines. The aim is to broaden the student rather than to give him field experience in his chosen career.

Of more immediate relevance to professional education are *co-op* and *internship* programs because they attempt to provide work for the student that is professionally enhancing. The co-op program, most widely used in engineering schools, involves one or two years of actual work as an engineer in a company during the four- or five-year undergraduate program. *Internship* refers to such a work period immediately following a period of formal education.

Professional schools have used the equivalent of the co-op program by having students do special work projects, internships, or regular work in an organization during the summer periods between the successive years of school or during a semester away from campus. For example, in the Sloan School of Management, students interested in becoming specialists in "planned change and organization development" are required, as part of their two-year master's program, to work in an organization as an organization-development intern during the summer between the first and second years. These jobs are paid, but they are jointly designed by the faculty and the employing organization to ensure that the work will be meaningful and that the supervisor will take on the responsibility of providing relevant feedback to each student. To make a program like this work, the school must establish relationships with a wide variety of organizations into which the students can be placed for the work period.

The Stanford Law School provides an opportunity for students in their fourth or fifth term to receive academic credit for a six-month period of operational training off campus (Ehrlich & Headrick, 1970). A strenuous effort is made by the faculty to ensure that these extern positions will be professionally valuable to the student. A faculty adviser arranges a program of work with the outside supervisor, decides what courses would be relevant to the student in the semester before entering the position, maintains contact with the student during the work period, and evaluates a research paper that the student is required to write on the basis of his experiences. Each extern is required to return to Stanford for at least one semester after the work period in order to ensure that he gains as much insight as possible from the experience. Positions have been found for students in administration of justice (juvenile and adult probation), land planning, trial courts, appellate courts, comparative law training, and administrative law. Some of the positions offer a salary to the extern during the summer months of his work period.

An effectively run co-op program solves many of the problems inherent in the effort to integrate basic science with clinical work. It gives the student an experience that is likely to be more real than can be provided locally as part of a practicum, and it gives the student a period of several months in which to try out his insights and skills, thus providing better opportunities for relevant feedback. The student is surrounded by practitioners in an environment where he can observe how professional practice actually operates. On the other hand, unless there is a close integration of the school faculty and the employing organization and unless care is taken to design the work carefully and provide relevant feedback, the learning goals of the program will not be met.

The *internship* model, as taken from medicine, specifies that the period of work shall occur after, rather than during, a period of formal education but is, in a sense, considered part of the educational process. Formal internships are usually arranged by the professional school and are run by organizations, whether hospitals, law offices, or businesses, as *educational* rather than *work* experiences. The educational character is usually symbolized by the extremely low wages the intern receives; by his graduation, after a specified period of time, out of the internship status; and by the specific kinds of work experiences based on specific learnings goals that are designed into the program. The effectiveness of internships depends upon the tasks that the intern is permitted to perform (the more real the better) and the amount and quality of the feedback he receives.

A special case of integrating work with study should be mentioned at this point because of its relevance to the training of those students who wish to pursue the more academic side of the professions. At MIT there is a program called Undergraduate Research Opportunities (UROP) which makes an effort to get departments to hire undergraduates down to the freshmen level as junior or senior research assistants in regular ongoing research projects (*Directory of MIT Undergraduate Research Opportunities,* 1971). The important element in the concept is getting the undergraduate involved in a more personal way with faculty and graduate students by giving him a regular job, a desk or a place of work, and a certain amount of responsibility commensurate with his ability. For many freshmen the initial job is at a very low level (e.g., "cleaning test-tubes"), but, as they learn more, they are given more responsibility so that, as juniors or seniors, they may be conducting their own pieces of research, designing equipment, or participating in the planning done by faculty and graduate students.

Opportunities such as these are typically available to graduate students in regular academic departments but are much rarer in professional schools, even though, as the knowledge base of professional practice generated by research widens, more students feel the need to learn about the research process. Recognizing that many of its students are interested in research and teaching or in careers for which they would benefit from research experiences beyond their own doctoral work, the Stanford Law School has started a program in which a limited number of third-year students receive a full year's academic credit towards a J.D. for working under the direction of two faculty members in an individualized program of research, specialized course work, and independent study (Ehrlich & Headrick, 1970). A student may apply to a pair of faculty members with whom he wants to work, or a faculty member who wishes to supervise students may notify the Faculty Committee on Interdisciplinary Studies and Research of his research interests. This committee has the responsibility of providing information to students concerning the research opportunities available to them and for developing new research opportunities.

Successful cooperative student-faculty research, intern programs, co-op work programs, and project-centered programs all require careful planning and substantial commitment of faculty and supervisors to ensure that the experience is professionally enriching to the student. They are at least as expensive as regular class work. But when one considers how different these programs are for the student, in his relationship to faculty, supervisors, the material itself, and his own role as an active rather than passive participant in the learning process, it is no wonder that students are increasingly demanding them. It is out of such experiences that they not only learn some of the professional skills but also gain some self-insight, some sense of the values and norms associated with professional roles, and some sense of the difficulties of relating to complex client systems. Thus, what may seem in the short run more expensive will probably in the long run be more economical because the student will learn more quickly and effectively how to perform competently and responsibly in the professional role.

Apprenticeships

MECHANISMS
APPLICABLE
TO THE EARLY
CAREER

The notion of *apprenticeship* adds two dimensions to what has previously been described as internship or cooperative types of programs. First, apprenticeship implies regular employment under senior professionals as part of earning one's license to practice; second, apprenticeship implies the possibility of gaining all one's learning from working with senior professionals without a period of formal professional school education. For example, though it is not too common, it is still possible for engineers and architects to obtain their license without attending college or professional school if they have worked long enough in an engineering or architectural office under the supervision of licensed professionals. This path is typically not available in medicine, but it is possible in law if the student can pass the bar examination.

The current trend seems to be to consider professional apprenticeships as periods of work that *immediately follow graduation* from professional school. The specific character of the apprenticeship therefore has important implications for the professional norms that are communicated to the young professional by the profession, especially in regard to career paths. If more role innovation is to be stimulated, the early career experiences must support whatever new concepts were learned in school. In some professions, what the professional school stimulates is out of line with what the apprenticeship allows. For example, architects are typically required to serve a three-year apprenticeship in an architectural office before being allowed to design and build anything on their own. Many graduates regard this practice as highly constricting and as forcing young architects into a traditional mold. Similarly, many young lawyers and managers find the initial jobs offered to them by companies or law offices to be too constricting and uninvolving.

An important difference between internship and apprenticeship is the nature of the supervision. In most internship situations the faculty of the school continues to play a feedback and evaluative role even if the student does his work outside the school. In the apprenticeship situation, the student is entirely evaluated by working professionals. The career options and the professional attitudes the student will develop are therefore strongly shaped by the apprenticeship opportunities that are available. A profession can perpetuate its traditions by limiting the kinds of early career opportunities that are available to graduates on their way to a license and by putting young professionals under supervision of very traditionally oriented senior professionals. One way to break out of such conservative traditions is to create alternative paths such as "halfway houses."

Career halfway houses, community service centers
In the halfway house, a person in transition from one role to another resides for a time in a house in which he is explicitly permitted to retain both roles. The concept has been most applicable in the transition from a hospital, especially a mental hospital, to a normal work routine. Patients can live for several weeks, months, or even years in a special residence with other discharged patients and with the reassurance of knowing that some of the staff of the house and the other ex-patients will remain supportive if outside stresses become too great. With such a base of support they can manage the stresses of a job and of daily life. As their strength grows they can leave the halfway house.

The role-innovative professional must have in the early part of his career a kind of "career halfway house" where the new conceptions gained in school continue to be supported in an actual job situation until the graduate gains enough self-confidence to pursue his innovative role on his own. The best example is, perhaps, Ralph Nader's Center for Responsive Law, where law students wishing to learn a new conception of how a lawyer might function can get experience and support through working on various of Nader's projects before moving on to careers of their own. Certain kinds of postdoctoral fellowships serve a similar purpose if the project on which the person is working facilitates his learning a new kind of professional role through providing contact with innovative professionals. As community centers in medicine, law, and architecture spring up under the auspices of local professional schools, work in such centers will also serve as a halfway house for postgraduate students. The essence of these various activities is that the young professional retains some link to his teachers while actually pursuing his job or apprenticeship. This link can serve as a counterweight to the traditional norms of professional practice unless, of course, the professional school itself is traditionally oriented. In our view, for role innovation to occur, there must be *both* a more flexible school and a more flexible set of early career paths. Neither element by itself will be sufficient.

Halfway houses can be used to introduce young professionals to the idea of an interdisciplinary service to clients. One model for such interdisciplinary work would be experience in Anne Roe's proposed "community resource center," which would combine within one agency a whole range of services such as health, legal, social work, psychiatric, financial, employment, budgetary, etc., for the entire age and socioeconomic range of the community (Roe, 1970). The benefit to apprentices would be the opportunity to work within an interdisciplinary team to learn from the outset how to integrate the different points of view of the different professionals involved. The University of Cincinnati has started a community design center that permits students and young professionals to become acquainted with the whole range of technical assistance needed by members of the community in improving their total environment. In the center, the actual professions represented are architecture, city planning, engineering, and law, and the projects already undertaken include advising residents on building repair, remodeling a teen center to bring it up to housing code requirements, designing a community health center for pediatrics, and starting a community art class and workshop in drafting for interested residents. The purpose of the center is clearly to help the community, but the involvement of students and young professionals provides educational opportunities as well ("Architect–Community Connections," undated).

In the area of medicine we can cite two examples. The Stanford Medical School has joined with a small community in developing a health center which involves collaborative work and planning by regular professionals, faculty members of the medical school, students, and community residents (Walsh, 1971). In New York City, the Martin Luther King Neighborhood Health Center provides medical, psychiatric, social service, and other kinds of counseling services to the members of a ghetto community by giving each family unit access to an interdisciplinary team involving various of the helping professions (Fry & Lech, 1971). Young professionals working with such a team clearly develop a different view of their career than those who start in a traditional residency.

The notion of the halfway house, especially as embodied in these interdisciplinary community centers, is probably one of the most important innovations to study and develop if the professions are to respond effectively to some of the forces we have cited.

Workshops and other concentrated postgraduate educational activities

Many of the insights into the role of the professional, the diagnosis of complex systems, the planning and managing of change projects, and the management of interprofessional teams can, perhaps, be learned only *after* the graduate is established in a professional career. He should be introduced to these ideas during professional school but, given the many barriers and resistances we have identified, it might in the end be more practical to make certain of the applied behavioral science and management components of the person's *continuing* education, supported by the professional association or the employing organization rather than the professional school.

The best example of such a program is the workshops run by the National Training Laboratories Institute of Applied Behavioral Science in Washington, D.C. General human relations, group dynamics, and leadership training are offered several times a year in different parts of the country for anyone wishing to attend. Many teachers, managers, nurses, and other professionals use such workshops to enhance their formal education. In addition, NTL has run focused programs to help professional groups with particular problems. For example, for several years NTL ran workshops for juvenile court judges, probation officers, and social workers to help them deliver a better-integrated service to the community. A major emphasis of this program was to help the judges, social workers, and probation officers to function as more of a *team*.

One argument in favor of a postgraduate approach is that the professional is more likely to realize the relevance of these areas after a few years of practice and is therefore more likely to be motivated to learn them at that time. With regard to group dynamics training, it has certainly been our observation in management school that students with a few years of experience in industry are much more motivated in these workshops or courses than students who have come straight out of college. One might assume that management training will become relevant only as the professional actually faces professional team problems or begins to think of a managerial role in his organization. For example, it has recently been recognized by the American College of Pathology that most senior pathologists administer fairly large laboratories and should, therefore, know something about administration. The college consequently has contracted with the University of Indiana Graduate School of Business to run one-week seminar-workshops for pathologists on the various aspects of management. The Radiological Association is presently looking into a similar venture for some of its members.

If the material to be covered cannot be designed into short workshops, another model is that of the Master of Public Health degree. Those professionals who wish to pursue a particular kind of career can attend an additional program for anywhere from three to twelve months to learn the new area. For example, one model for human relations training centers in universities might be to offer basic applied behavioral and social training to lawyers, doctors, social workers, architects, or any other professional group wishing to avail itself of that opportunity.[12] Such training would typically come after completion of all formal professional training. One can see the relevance of such a postgraduate course in applied behavioral science, sociology, and urbanology for all those professionals who intend to pursue a career in community health, legal, or design services.

---

[12] The Human Relations Training Center at Boston University has recently renamed itself the Applied Social Science Center and is developing a postgraduate social science program for professionals.

We have reviewed above a number of different kinds of mechanisms that can be used during and after the professional's formal education as a way of loosening up the present educational and early career system. These mechanisms in one way or another vary the student's relationship to the teacher, to other students, to the material to be learned, to the physical setting, to the time dimension, and to the evaluation or grading system used. They can be used singly or in combinations as experimental vehicles to develop some flexibility in the educational process by creating some alternatives for educators to look at comparatively.

We reviewed (1) self-paced study; (2) independent study; (3) concentrated study; (4) seminar-tutorial methods; (5) project- or problem-centered study; (6) practicum or clinical courses; (7) co-op, work-study, off-campus study, and internship programs; and (8) postgraduate mechanisms like apprenticeships, career halfway houses, community service centers, workshops, and postgraduate regular study in other fields.

Each of the mechanisms described has been used in different settings with varying degrees of initial success and long-range viability. They are not presented here as *the* answer nor as a catalogue of educational innovations. For example, we covered none of the possibilities that arise from the more creative use of educational technology such as films, videotape, audiotape, computer-aided instruction, etc. The mechanisms we reviewed are presented in an effort to stretch the thinking of the reader and to aid the diagnostic process of those professors or administrators in professional schools who are beginning to feel the unfreezing pressures and who are casting about for alternatives. As we said in our chapter on planned change, one cannot *tell* members of another organization what to do, but one can facilitate their diagnosis of themselves and can provide alternatives for them to think about to help them scan their envionment in search of a solution that fits their particular needs.

11. Some Bold Horizons: A New Kind of Professional Education

In the previous chapters we have reviewed what is needed, some of the barriers to the introduction of educational innovation, and some of the mechanisms that may overcome those barriers. In this final chapter, we would like to think a bit more boldly. If one were really to redesign the professional school, how might one organize it for more effective and economical professional education? How might one educate tomorrow's professional to truly prepare him for the challenges that will face him? In answering these questions, we are clearly going beyond our data and speculating about future possibilities. Our proposals should be viewed as a set of best guesses about what will be needed, but we recognize full well some of the problems and pitfalls inherent in the proposed changes. Much of what we propose is already being tried in piecemeal fashion, but we are not aware of any integrative efforts which combine some of the innovations that are today technologically and economically feasible.

Development of a genuinely different and more responsive professional education would require four major changes: (1) new kinds of learning modules built on better theories of how students learn; (2) new kinds of faculty members who bring different skills, attitudes, and values to their job; (3) new kinds of administrative structures and procedures that are more flexible and that adapt to the learning tasks to be met; and (4) perpetual self-diagnosis and evaluation research.

To summarize the argument before we discuss each point: the new professional school would start with a learning theory that integrates basic sciences, applied sciences, and professional skills within single learning modules rather than separating them into successive "core courses," "applied courses," and "practicum." The new professional school would be organized around learning modules of varying lengths and would permit the putting together of different patterns of modules, dealing with different professional career foci, leading to different kinds of professional degrees which would require different lengths of time to complete. The new professional school would have a small permanent faculty and a large part-time adjunct faculty to permit the offering of a wide variety of modules to students. Adjunct professors would function as consultants, teaching at several schools and possibly maintaining some private practice as well. They would have power in determining school policy and in the design of the curriculum, however, and they would do research on a *full-time* basis every third or fourth year. Physically, the new professional school would be organized around a learning resource center that should include as many laboratories and applications-oriented subcenters as possible, much like a teaching hospital that is tied closely into various community service activities.

Administratively the school would be highly decentralized, using only those information and control procedures that would facilitate the student's learning process and keep track of information about the student that he and his future employers really need. Such an information system should be built with the involvement of future employers and students and should *not* be designed to service the school administration primarily. Finally, the school should deliberately avoid the search for standardized solutions to curriculum questions, engaging instead in a perpetual process of self-diagnosis and research on the outcomes of its educational efforts. Such educational research should be supported by the professional associations and should include efforts to evaluate the appropriateness and quality of the professional services being offered to clients.

ELEMENT 1: NEW LEARNING MODULES Professional education must be organized around a new kind of learning module which (1) is flexible enough to accommodate students with different learning styles; (2) integrates the basic science, applied science, and skill elements to be learned; (3) costs less than present comparable educational modules (courses); (4) increases the amount learned by students; and (5) encourages students to "learn how to learn," so that they will be more able to continue their own education following formal schooling. Such modules should also be flexible enough to facilitate the continuing education of alumni of the school at varying periods following graduation and as career switches may be desired.

Why seek such new modules?

1   The development of new kinds of learning modules would take better advantage of what we already know about the learning process in young and middle-aged adults and would stimulate further study of how people learn. The learning process must be better understood before we can invent lower-cost education without reducing the potential for learning (Kolb, 1971).

2   The cost of education must be brought down without reverting to the standard oversimplifications of substituting lectures, books, or audio-visual devices on a massive scale for seminars, apprenticeships, tutorials, and other forms of education that are, by present accounting methods, indeed more expensive. We must invent new kinds of learning settings and new methods of interaction between students and subject material, and students and faculty. The module concept can help stimulate such invention by emphasizing a learning unit of variable size, sometimes smaller and sometimes larger than a course, but smaller than an entire curriculum.

3   Many colleges and universities have concluded that the present system of courses organized by semesters or quarters and tied together into a curriculum of some years' duration does *not* produce optimal levels of learning. Whenever schools have experimented with a more flexible timetable and more learning options for students, they have concluded that more learning has taken place. The major difficulty has been greater cost and greater difficulty of getting faculty to work in a more flexible system. We need a new kind of unit that is not as autonomous as a course nor as total as a curriculum. Such a unit, here called a module, could involve *several* faculty members, be of varying duration, and have any of a number of different learning goals or involve any of a number of different learning methods.

4   If professional education is to become more flexible, permit interruption, and permit preparation for a variety of career paths, it must consist of learning modules that can be put together in a

variety of ways for a variety of purposes, leading to a variety of degrees.

How are such modules to be designed?
New learning modules could be organized on one of several bases; (1) *functionally* by area to be learned (this would make them similar to our present system of *courses*); (2) by *skill level* in which each level would have basic science, applied science, and practicum components but at different levels of student competence; (3) by *area of practice or type of career* to be pursued, in which each module would be slanted toward work with a given client system or toward a particular set of skills that the student wished to develop, but again each module would involve a mix of basic science, applied science, and practicum. Since the essence of the module concept is to combine and integrate the basic science, applied science, and practicum components, only the latter two bases for organizing modules should really be given serious consideration.

The focus in design should be on the nature of the learning *process.* Thus the four design questions to be asked are: (1) What basic sciences does the student need to learn, and how are these best learned? (2) What applied sciences does the student need to learn, and how are these best learned? (3) What specific skills, attitudes, and values does the student need to learn, and how are these best learned? (4) How are these *learning processes* best integrated, considering the problems of maximizing learning at a minimum cost?

Educational innovators often err in trying to integrate learning *materials* from different disciplines or levels of difficulty rather than considering how to integrate learning *methods.* Thus curriculum planners look at blocks of material to be covered and consider how they can be arranged, shortened, combined, etc., but they rarely ask how lectures, small groups, concentrated study, fieldwork, tutoring, projects, and independent study can be combined and integrated. It is our hypothesis that the integration of basic, applied, and skill components can only work if we first ask how the *methods* which are suitable for each of these areas can be integrated. For example, basic materials might be best covered by reading, live lectures, taped lectures or films, self-paced study, or programmed instruction. Applied areas require the involvement of practitioners and the opportunity to at least observe cases; thus they require workshops, practicum courses, simulations, seminars, projects, and other methods that permit more active involvement of students. Skill practice requires active participation by students and good feedback on how the student is doing; thus we need to think in terms of internships, apprenticeships, and other activities that involve actual client contact. We believe that we can combine these elements creatively and thus facilitate an integration of basic, applied, and skill components of professional education.

The design should be invented jointly by faculty *teams* that represent the main areas of concern: basic science, applied science, and practicum. If possible, applied behavioral scientists should be part of the team to facilitate the integration of behavioral science *content* as well as to aid in the invention of the module. The applied behavioral scientist is most likely to have thought about the theory and practice of learning and teaching, and to be sensitive to the problems of teamwork among several faculty members.

The initial design focus should be on analysis of how students *learn,* not on how to teach something. The question should then be considered of what alternative technologies or methods are available to facilitate the learning processes that have been identified. At this point, the team should consider (1) a wide range of alternative methods (with help from the behavioral scientist) such as the ones identified above; (2) when and how to use peers, more advanced students, junior faculty, senior faculty, clinical professors, practitioners, and other human resources; and, most important of all, (3) how to integrate the use of materials, the computer, the library, and the various student and faculty resources.

The design team must resist the impulse to take *one* element such as the computer or the interdisciplinary seminar and push it to some extreme form, because the answer to better and lower-cost education will lie in inventing ways to *integrate the use of various different kinds of resources.* Such integration will be possible only if faculty teams take the time to analyze the process of learning that underlies what they do and then ask whether there are alternative and better ways to learn the same thing.[1]

---

[1] We know of at least three examples at MIT in which interdisciplinary teams have designed new educational formats by sitting together and planning for many months, learning each other's biases, and finally seeking a solution that would integrate their biases into a new solution rather than a compromise — i.e., the USSP and ESG programs mentioned in Chapter 10 and an interdisciplinary program focusing on science, engineering, and the humanities ("Concourse," 1971).

As a first approximation of what such modules might look like, one can take a combination of the components which are presently taught in sequence and consider how to interlace them. Thus, in the first month of school, the medical student might be exposed to some patients, have access to a computer-aided diagnostic system to check his own diagnostic skill, attend a series of videotaped lectures on basic anatomy, physiology, and any other basic science material needed to aid diagnosis, join a small group discussion or seminar on basic conceptual material (such as the concepts of *normality, health,* etc.), join a workshop group focused on gaining self-insight through analysis of feelings generated by patient contact, have access to a concentrated study course in diagnostic techniques supplemented by a library of readings and computer-aided instructional packages on the symptomatology of different diseases, attend clinical conferences at which therapeutic measures are discussed, and so on.

After a month, the student might be given some patients of his own and join a group devoted to the systematic analysis of physician-client contact. Such a group would focus not only on the medical aspects—when and how to make a diagnosis and decide on a therapeutic intervention—but also on the interpersonal and psychological aspects—what feelings are generated by having responsibility for the health of another human being, how to ask questions in a helpful manner, how to deal with patient anxiety, hostility, resistance, etc., and so on. In such groups, the help of an applied behavioral scientist would be especially relevant. Instruction in the basic sciences would continue throughout, but, because much of this material would be on tape, in libraries, or in self-paced units, students could concentrate on it when they were psychologically ready to do so. Each month would repeat more or less the same combination of methods but at a deeper level of analysis. As students developed basic knowledge and skills, they could take optional learning modules focused on specialities they wished to pursue. Again, each module would contain some patient contact, some small group discussion of relevant issues, some concentrated study, basic material in reading or lecture form, and some workshops dealing with the learning process itself.

Another example of integrating learning methods is the two-week full-time live-in workshop designed to teach group dynamics to participants. The designers of a workshop typically spend two to three full days planning the content to be covered and the actual design to be used, when the design issue is how to combine (a) practicum time in which learners have a chance to learn about "here-and-now" group behavior, (b) focused exercises that illustrate vividly some of the concepts to be learned (this would be comparable to laboratory study in the sciences) and that permit learners to practice new kinds of behaviors, and (c) purely conceptual material that may be provided through lectures, readings, films, or videotapes (Schein & Bennis, 1965).

The model that underlies this kind of workshop assumes that learning is a cyclical activity that starts with concrete experience, is followed by a period of reflective observation (which may or may not involve group discussion to share observations and inferences), is then followed by a period of abstract conceptualization (usually aided by formal input of some sort from the teacher), and then closes with an effort at generalization which typically involves trying out new behavior which in turn produces new experience, thus setting the cycle in motion once again (Kolb, 1971). Though this theory has been applied most frequently to behavioral and social science learning, there is no reason to doubt its applicability to the more abstract and "hard" sciences. In fact, the proponents of project-centered study are using a learning theory very similar to the one described.

Ultimately, the important issue in creating new learning modules is to give up the artificial constraints imposed by traditional higher education methods and calendars. The modules do not have to be of any given length; they do not have to be standardized; they do not have to involve permanent in-house faculty or be taught by single, autonomous professors; they do not even have to be offered on campus.[2] They do not have to involve lectures, readings, and examinations, and they do not have to carry a certain number of units or credits. It may be inconvenient during a transition period

---

[2] Some of the more innovative models of the use of television are exemplified in the programs of the University of South Africa and the British Open University. In both cases student groups spend only a short time on campus, doing most of their learning by themselves or in study groups that are operated regionally and tied together by visiting professors or by closed-circuit broadcasted lectures and discussion topics. Materials are mailed out from the central administrative headquarters and assignments done by students on their own time are graded there. Videotapes or movies could be similarly used if one had a decentralized student body and regional learning resource centers that could provide a library, study space, tutorial help, or whatever other services students needed (Marais, 1970; Maclure, 1971).

to give up the various props that our traditions provide, but we should recognize that there is no *inherent* validity in the present higher education system. Professional schools are in a particularly good position to be innovative because they often have a degree of autonomy not enjoyed by regular departments.

Some special foci for new modules

Professional schools should introduce *optional* modules dealing explicitly with the professional's ability to (1) function as a generalist as well as a specialist, (2) function as a member of an intra- or interprofessional team, (3) function as a project manager of intra- or interprofessional teams.

As we have previously argued, client systems are becoming more complex and can only be dealt with by complex teams. It is also clear that all the professions are becoming more and more differentiated and specialized. In order to match the client system with the right mix of professionals, therefore, we will need to develop a new kind of interprofessional G.P. who can work with the client system on a preliminary diagnosis involving the selection of the right professional specialties for the final project work. A good example of such a G.P. role may be found in architecture and planning projects in which the small planning consulting firm does the initial diagnosis of a complex problem such as the design of a campus or an urban transportation system, and, with the client, then decides what kind of architects, planners, lawyers, economists, engineers, etc., will be needed to develop the system and build it. The initial diagnostic phase may last from one month to one year. The planning consultant's job is to make a good diagnosis and to know where the right set of professional specialists can be found to work on the problem once it has been well-defined.

We have also pointed out that interprofessional teams will be effective only if their members have been trained to be both skilled members and skilled managers. The management skills required to create a team, build its effectiveness, maximize its resources, and then disband it when the project is finished *can be taught.* One portion is covered by the introduction of the behaviorial sciences into professional curricula. If sensitivity training is introduced and if courses on group dynamics are taught, students will learn about groups and how to function in them. Such learning will not ensure any insight into the managerial side of the issue, however. Effective project management of interdisciplinary teams will also require some understanding of finance, law, public policy, and other more traditional areas of administration.

The focus on management should be given especially serious attention because of the increasing evidence that in most professions, even the academic profession, managerial responsibilities are acquired by all professionals in the normal course of their careers. This happens faster in some fields than others—e.g., engineering—but it tends to happen in most of them sooner or later. It would be highly desirable to develop modules which would not only introduce the beginning student to managerial issues at an elementary level, but also be available to practicing professionals when the need arises for them to make a transition to administration in one form or another. Instead of learning management on an ad hoc and haphazard basis, it would be much more desirable if the engineer could sign up at his local professional school or area learning-resource center and take management modules as part of his continuing education. We previously pointed out that the American College of Pathology is offering such modules to its members. Perhaps professional associations in combination with professional schools are the ideal sponsors for the development of more modules like these.

To introduce these types of modules, faculty members from neighboring departments or universities must be brought into the professional school on a part-time basis to work with the regular school faculty to develop the right kind of module. The length and content of the module will vary from profession to profession. Some professions, such as engineering and architecture, are facing team and managerial issues in the immediate future and should begin to develop such modules right away. Other professions, such as teaching, seem to have less immediate need, though one could certainly do a better job of integrating the concerns of the educational and hospital administrators with those of the teachers and doctors.

Module sets, career flexibility, and degree flexibility

If different kinds of modules can be invented, it becomes possible to create for students a more flexible set of paths through professional school—reflecting their different career interests—and to create for professors opportunities to teach in a style that particularly suits them. The present system of elective courses is supposed to function this way, but courses are often too long and too theory-oriented to provide the kind of flexible practicum variation which, for example, would differentiate the student going into a specialty, general practice, urban community services, research, administration, and/or teaching. For each of these careers one ought to develop module *sets* that put a high premium on integrating the basic science, applied science, and practicum aspects which pertain to that particular career alternative.

One approach to this problem has been described in the Princeton study of education for environmental design (Geddes & Spring, 1967). A team at the Princeton School of Architecture set out to define the task of environmental design and to come up with a national framework for environmental education. In describing the design task, they came up with three basic elements: (1) the design decision-making process; (2) the scope of the work to be done; and (3) the scale set by the physical boundaries of the problem. These three elements were further divided into 216 task descriptions, each dealing with a different aspect of the design process. Out of the range of these different aspects, they distilled nine distinct types of educational programs from which different schools could choose. The academic training period was divided into six time modules so that students could shift from one type of program to another at the end of two-year periods. This would relieve schools of the burden of trying to cover all aspects of the design process and allow students to put the emphasis of their training on the particular aspects of design on which they wanted to focus.

The degrees given to students should become similarly flexible, reflecting the particular set of modules the student has taken. Several steps in this direction have recently been taken. The Carnegie Commission has recommended differentiating the Ph.D. as a research degree from a Doctor of Arts, which would be essentially a teaching degree (Spurr, 1970). The Stanford Law School, recognizing the need for more types of degrees, now offers, in addition to the standard Doctor of Jurisprudence (J.D.) for students intending to practice law, an advanced Doctor of Juristic Science (J.S.D.) in law or in a combination of fields. This degree normally takes two years of study beyond the J.D. For students who wish to continue for one year beyond the J.D. or for students who are having difficulty completing the J.S.D. requirements, a terminal Master of Science in Law (J.S.M.) is available. Finally, for students who do not necessarily wish to practice as lawyers but who desire some training in law, there is a Master of Jurisprudence degree, requiring two years of study, and there are joint degree programs with economics and political science (Ehrlich & Headrick, 1970). At Sherbrook University in Quebec, students wishing to go into hospital, educational, or industrial management take some of their course work in the School of Management and some in the Medical School or in the School of Education, leading to differentiated management degrees based on some common and some differentiated courses.

A further step in the right direction would be to certify the completion of modules in some more formal fashion to permit easier interruption of education and the geographical movement from one region to another. For example, the new differentiation of degrees at the Stanford Law School allows students to terminate their legal education at a variety of levels, from a nonprofessional J.M. degree to an advanced dissertation and research degree. At any of these points, the student can leave school holding a degree that recognizes what he has accomplished (not as a dropout), making it relatively easy for him to switch to another field, reenter at a later period, or enter a career for which he is prepared.

Part of the argument behind new differentiation of degrees is that professionals such as lawyers and doctors are overtrained for many of their jobs and that there is a growing need to put more paraprofessionals into practice in response to the needs of society and the desire of students to engage in meaningful activities earlier. However, if the proliferation of degrees is not to become a new source of rigidity, it will be important to permit easier access to various sets of modules through looser admission criteria.

All the above hinge on a set of faculty attitudes and an administrative structure that do not exist in today's professional school. We must turn next to this topic to indicate what kinds of changes might be visualized if our modular concept is to be workable.

ELEMENT 2: A NEW KIND OF FACULTY The professor who could invent and function in modules of the sort we have described must have as his most important characteristic a deep concern for the learning process in addition to the concern for the development of his discipline through research. Professors vary as to whether their primary commitment is to the development of their discipline or to the development of their students. Among those who are committed to students we find two further types—those who feel that students benefit most if they are *taught,* with emphasis on the teaching activities of the professor, and those who feel that students benefit most if they are stimulated to *learn,* with emphasis on the learning process conceived of as a complex transaction between teacher, student, and whatever is to be learned. For the innovations we are calling for here, only the last-named type of professor will detach himself sufficiently from his content and past teaching style to be able to think about the learning needs of different kinds of students in different kinds of circumstances. In other words, the *professor must become more learning-centered* rather than teaching-centered.

A *second* prime characteristic that will be needed and is relatively rare among today's professoriat is the *ability to function as a leader or member of a team.* It is our belief that we cannot integrate the basic, applied, and practical elements in the new modules unless the professors who ordinarily would be teaching the different elements can get together, share their perspectives and attitudes about both content and learning theory, and develop enough mutual trust and communication to be able to go beyond compromise solutions to genuine new integrations of their points of view. As we have mentioned, the training of the professor tends to high-light autonomy and to play down teamwork, hence the new kind of professor either has to have been socialized in a different kind of graduate school or must learn the skills of teamwork sometime during his career. Such learning is possible if the members accept the common task as real and important and if applied behavioral scientists are available to help in this learning process. This assertion is based on three years' experience as Undergraduate Planning Professor at MIT, when I sat on innumerable problem-solving and planning committees dealing with curriculum matters and other academic problems. I found that my participation was of most use to the committee if I played a "process consultant" role designed to help members of the committee be more effective as group members and to help the entire committee be more effective by encouraging frequent reviews of how it was working and how these processes could be improved upon (Schein, 1969, 1970*a*).

A *third* element that will be needed in professors of the sort we have in mind is *knowledge of the psychology and sociology of learning.* Most professors I have encountered either don't know the rudiments of learning theory or unconsciously ignore what they know. The outcome is that the typical classroom situation in college or professional school almost completely fails to take advantage of what has been learned over the last 50 years about how people learn. A great deal is known about the varieties of learning depending upon what is to be learned; the age of the learner; the motivation or cognitive style of the learner; the social setting in which learning is to take place; the motivation, attitudes, or style of the teacher; the pacing of material; the use of different forms and timing of feedback; and so on. Most professors tend to have only a rudimentary theory of learning and one that is likely to be based only on their own past experience and that of colleagues in their own discipline.

To give but one example, almost all learning theories put great emphasis on the need for the learner to make some response which leads to some feedback or information as to the results of his response, which, in turn, leads to a better response. Yet most college courses put a student into a passive listening and reading situation for the better part of a semester and then ask him for a single global response in the form of a test or a paper to be written. They then provide feedback only in the form of a global evaluation such as a grade. Since there is typically no second chance, there is no incentive to use whatever feedback information was provided. If we used the learning theory, we would assign *multiple drafts* of the paper or demand frequent responses throughout the term so that the feedback could be used during the course to improve performance. In the typical course, the feedback is too little and too late.

The strong disciplinary orientation of most professors makes them more responsive to what has been written about the teaching of their particular area than what is known about learning in general. We will have to find a way to reeducate professors and to get them interested in the general problem of learning and what is known about the learning process, possibly through focused workshops on learning.

I have run several seminars on teaching and have found that one model that works is to start with group interviews of teachers rather than formal material on learning theory. A group of interested faculty could get together once a week and each week interview one of their members or a guest on his teaching goals, his preferred style, how he deals with certain problems, etc. Out of a series of such interviews, we typically were able to induce some of the common and important elements of the learning process. The diversity of styles was usually dramatic, however, which forced each participant to question whether his own style was valid in some absolute sense, as he had previously assumed. Once there was recognition of diversity and a sense of the common elements that all teachers faced, it was easier to introduce some formal learning theory. I found very little resistance to the ideas of the group interviews. Most visitors or seminar members were anxious to share their thoughts about teaching and felt that the experience of being forced to articulate these thoughts was very helpful to them (Schein, 1967).

A *fourth* element that will be needed in professors is *greater interest in and skill in occupational counseling and advising of students.* If the professional school becomes more flexible, a greater burden is put upon both students and professors to think through what the right path is for any given student. We have seen efforts of loosening up the freshman year at MIT that stood or fell on the quality of student advising. The student could not think through the bewildering set of options and make good choices among them. A different kind of attitude from faculty advisers was needed—an attitude of interest and concern for the career of the student combined with some skill in establishing a viable relationship with the student such that a real exchange could take place between them. We have tried short workshops on advising to which large numbers of faculty were invited and have found MIT faculty are greatly interested in such workshops (McIntyre & Rubin, 1969).

A *fifth* and very important element that combines several of the above is that the faculty member must *like and respect people*—students, his colleagues, and the clients for whom the professional education is ultimately designed. We are now referring partly to an attitude and partly to a personality characteristic, hence it is not easy to guess whether professors can learn in this area or whether professors with these characteristics will have to be found by means of selection. It seems clear, however, that the invention and operation of a flexible modular system will require interpersonal commitments of all sorts and that professors who prefer autonomous, solitary, scholarly pursuits would find such a system very uncomfortable.

A *sixth,* and final, element is that the professor must himself have *tendencies toward role innovation.* There is very little incentive in today's professional school to "rock the boat." The system is thoroughly bureaucratized and basically comfortable both for faculty and students. Unless a professor has strong motivation to innovate, he will not have the emotional energy to go through the change process required to convert to a new system and then to keep the new system going in the face of regressive forces.

In summary, the kind of faculty needed in a new kind of professional school built around flexible, integrated modules will be learning-centered and knowledgeable about learning principles, capable of working in team settings, interpersonally competent and positive toward people, concerned about the career development of students, and role-innovative.

Where and how is such a faculty to be found?
Most professional schools already have faculty members who fit the above description, but such professors are often neutralized in their innovative efforts by other less innovative professors or are defeated by the bureaucratic difficulties of innovating within a traditional academic structure. One way to offset such restraining forces is for the academic administration to give more support and encouragement to the role innovators and to give some protection to innovations while they are in a young and vulnerable condition.

One possible though not necessarily desirable mechanism for stimulating more role innovators would be to discontinue the tenure system, because it gives a great deal of power to older professors and is sometimes seen as a way of perpetuating traditional, rather than innovative, attitudes. For example, Hampshire College, a new undergraduate liberal arts college, has no tenure system but hires professors on three- to seven-year contracts. The review committee for reappointment consists of faculty and students ("Hampshire College," November 27, 1970).

Most schools, when they hire new faculty, can choose whether to pay attention only to the intellectual-scholarly criteria or whether to consider attitudes and traits such as those mentioned above. A second way, then, of finding this new kind of faculty is to build the above criteria explicitly into the selection process.[3] It is my impression that among current crops of Ph.D. students in all fields, there is less enthusiasm for basic research and more interest

---

[3] A step that has recently been taken in this direction is to involve students in the selection of teachers. At the University of Alabama, prospective professors are interviewed by a group of students as well as by other faculty at the school (Scully, 1971).

in teaching and in finding new ways of organizing the learning process. If this trend is real and if the schools take the trouble to search out the role innovators, there should be no lack of candidates.

The third way to get this new kind of faculty is through deliberate retraining of the present faculty. This is the most difficult alternative but is still feasible if the retraining is done in a sympathetic and supportive fashion, taking account of the characteristics of professors and the likelihood of arousing defensiveness if it is even suggested that some new attitudes might be more appropriate for the professional school of the future (Schein, 1970a). As I have indicated above, I have been involved in several efforts in which genuine attitude change was brought about from a position of conservativism and dogmatism about teaching to one of openness and a spirit of inquiry. Recent student unrest has helped to unfreeze many professors who now recognize that *something* is wrong, but who need help in making the diagnosis of just what it is that is wrong and how their own behavior may be part of the problem.

Part-time and adjunct faculty

As the professions become more highly differentiated, the number of specialties that will have to be covered in any professional education will increase greatly. Similarly, if the professional schools are to become more transdisciplinary and to use the behavorial and social sciences more effectively, they will have to sit on a broader and broader intellectual base. It will obviously not be possible for a given professional school to hire on a full-time basis all the specialists it needs to cover the various modules it should make available to students. On the other hand, professional schools have not had much luck having their students take courses in other departments because such courses are typically not geared to the special problems of the profession. A better solution for broadening the base is to carry a much larger faculty, but to carry a large percentage of it on a part-time or adjunct basis. The professors with particular specialties might work for two or more geographically dispersed professional schools while still spending enough time in each school to sense what the specific learning needs are in that school. The Union Graduate School, which we discussed in more detail in an earlier section, has a relatively small full-time core faculty in residence at the headquarters in Yellow Springs, Ohio. In addition, at each center there are full- and part-time adjunct faculty who are equally involved with students in the design and implementation of their programs but who may maintain outside activities as well. Finally, some special adjunct faculty make themselves available for the duration of a single student's program that is particularly interesting to them.

Adjunct faculty must exist in sufficient numbers within a school so that they do not become second-class citizens. They must be given a role in the administration of the school and the planning of the modularized curriculum to ensure their sense of membership in that community and they must be promoted on the basis of new kinds of criteria which take into account their part-time status. However, there is no reason why such professors could not enjoy membership in two or three communities without losing involvement in any of them. We know of several behavioral scientists who divide their time between two or three universities and carry on a private consulting practice. There is no reason why the same concept could not be applied to a professor of environmental law or community mental health or some other area that is needed in each of several schools. The adjunct-professor role would also facilitate the employment of women who can only work part-time.

One important by-product of a part-time faculty is that the professor is constantly importing into one system things he has learned in the other systems he is a part of, with the result that each of the schools benefits from a constant flow of new ideas. The problems of absenteeism only arise if we define *part-time* in terms of the present calendar of being on campus one or two days per week. If we think of a modularized system, a part-time professor might be at one school for two months and a different school for two months, etc., but he would be full-time on that school's activities while he is in residence.

ELEMENT 3: A NEW ADMINISTRATIVE STRUCTURE AND ACADEMIC CALENDAR One of the subtlest but most powerful conservative forces in professional schools (and universities generally) is the whole administrative set of routines that revolve around (1) the academic calendar; (2) the recording of what students have taken, what grades and credits have been received; and (3) the day-to-day management of the faculty, support personnel, and students of the school.

Because of the large number of students to be "processed," there is a strong tendency to develop systems of registration and record keeping that are dominated by criteria of efficiency rather than relevance to learning. Similarly, because of the divisionalizing of the curriculum into disciplines, there is a strong tendency to develop an academic calendar based on criteria of efficient coordination of different courses rather than criteria of how long any given course really ought to be in terms of what is to be learned. Most faculty members are emotionally dependent upon the calendar as a way of structuring their work and would be highly uncomfortable if they had a free choice of how long their course ought to be from year to year. However, if the new modular concept is to have any chance of working, the faculty would have to reopen all the questions pertaining to administrative procedures, admission criteria, schedules, and calendars, because different modules would be of differing lengths and intensities.

One example of an existing program is the School of Education at the University of Massachusetts, which offers a program of modularized courses outside of the regular course offerings, with a special administrative office to handle registration of credits. The aim of this program is to provide greater flexibility for both students and faculty in the design and choice of educational experiences. A standard university credit consists of 15 modules of credit. Students choose educational experiences ranging from one-hour seminars to off-campus activities such as classroom teaching or observing to multiple-week courses to intensive weekend learning seminars. For each experience they receive an appropriate number of credit modules which, at the end of the term, are converted into standard credit units. Since the modular credits are automatically registered with the administrative office, the student need not even register until the end of the semester, when his credit is converted. One such course on science education consists of 55 different offerings which the student can package in any way he sees fit. Such a course allows the student the choice of a fully consolidated, long-term experience or a series of one-shot events with multiple entry and exit points as he wishes (Christensen, 1971).

One might also envision a program that starts with a week of concentrated study dealing with an overview of the entire curriculum and the choices available within it. Following this there might be a one- or two-month period in which two or three basic modules would be taken; followed by two or three months of elective modules; followed by a workshop on problems of client relations, planned change, and teamwork for all students; followed by another period of elective modules, and so on. It is an empirical question whether certain modules should be standardized in length and whether portions of the academic year should therefore be structured. Furthermore, much more frequent reviews of the entire structure would have to be built into the administrative system so that it could change as the learning material changes.

As to the matter of record keeping, credits, and grades, these should be organic to what is being covered and to the needs of the student and his future employers for information relevant to career decisions. Inherent in the design of a module is a statement of the goals to be achieved by that module. Those goals generally can be translated into a set of performance criteria that should determine how to measure student performance. In many cases this criterion will be knowledge and problem-solving skill which has been accumulated and which can be measured by actual test performance as in the case of programmed texts. In other cases students will have to perform some activity and be judged by faculty as to the skill exhibited and rated. The important point would be to develop multidimensional performance evaluation systems that permit the faculty member to describe the student's accomplishments in concrete terms rather than in vague letter grades (Elbow, 1969). Students should be involved in setting these performance criteria, since they often know better what measure will determine whether or not they really know something or really have acquired a certain skill or attitude. Future employers should also be involved in determining criteria since they know best what they are *really* looking for as a basis of hiring, but they should not control this process since such control would reintroduce conservative forces from the profession.

To make such a system operate faculty and students must be actively involved in all administrative affairs, since administrative procedures interact so strongly with the learning system. Such involvement presupposes the kind of learning-centered professor we have previously described. If such a faculty is available, it becomes possible to subordinate the administrative concerns to those of the learning system and to develop administrative procedures that can be easily changed as the total learning system is redesigned from year to year. Above all, a tendency to standardize the administrative procedures must be avoided. Once they are standardized, it becomes all too easy to adapt the learning modules to the existing procedures rather than redesign the modules when they need redesign—even if that means differing lengths of time, different systems of keeping records, and different systems of measuring student performance.

ELEMENT 4: PERPETUAL SELF-DIAGNOSIS AND EVALUATION RESEARCH It is a frequent observation that organizations tend toward stability. Indeed the very concept of creating an organization means, at some level, standardizing roles, dividing labor, and developing formal procedures for task or goal accomplishment. At the same time, it has become more and more evident that in the rapidly changing environment of today it is critical for organizations to develop flexibility and self-renewal mechanisms. Schools, universities, and professional schools are especially in need of self-renewal, as we have argued; thus the question arises of how one goes about providing for that self-renewal.

The answer is basically simple: by institutionalizing a process of perpetual self-diagnosis and evaluation research in order to keep a flow of information coming into the school—information that will permit it to judge its performance against its goals. The force toward change is then the gap between what is wanted and what is achieved, combined with skillful diagnosis to determine how to adapt the system to achieve the goals. This logic dictates that the diagnosis and evaluation research be done by members of the school with *help* from outsiders, but that it not be farmed out to professional researchers or diagnosticians. This point is crucial because it is essential that all members of the faculty, administration, and student body learn how to evaluate outcomes and how to make diagnoses. If this skill is not learned by members of the system that is trying to manage the change, they may be unhappy with the results of evaluation studies but won't know how to do any better.

Evaluation research should be long-range as well as short-range. For example, a given module may have certain goals. After some tries it ought to be determined how well the module is achieving those goals. However, on a longer-range basis the school has a certain mission, an ideal of what its graduates ought to be doing in their careers. It is therefore essential that evaluation research include studies of alumni to determine what career paths they have followed, where they have ended up, what their views of their professional education are, what experiences led them to different kinds of careers within a profession, who has become a role innovator and why, and so on.

Even more important would be evaluation research on professional practice itself. In many professions the competence of the practitioner is extremely difficult to determine, yet virtually no research is conducted to assess whether the client is getting good service or not. Perhaps the outstanding example is architecture, in which the criteria for design competence are very vague once one gets past simple criteria like safety and permanence of the structure.[4] If the professions could develop their own evaluative systems and do more self-diagnosis, this would have a salutary effect on professional education in making it clearer what kinds of competence and attitudes are really critical for effective professional performance.

Good models of evaluation research and diagnosis are difficult to find, and within each profession the model is probably going to be different. We do believe, however, that inherent in the theories of planned change (Chapters 8 and 9) are general models which could be adapted to a given profession and which could lead to "action research" that would provide useful data on the effectiveness of that profession (Sanford, 1970).

We have defined some elements of what may be regarded as a utopian concept — a professional school organized around modules which integrate basic, applied, and skill components; run by an innovative, largely part-time faculty who are expert in learning theory, teamwork, and interpersonal skills; administered flexibly with heavy involvement from students, faculty, and future employers; constantly evaluating itself, its output, and the effectiveness of the profession itself through perpetual self-diagnosis and evaluation research. Such a school should at least be tried out — if it has the characteristics we have specified, it can easily go back to some version of the old system. It is our conviction that in a rapidly changing, turbulent world, it will be the adaptive type of system such as we have described that will be both the cheapest and the most effective way of educating tomorrow's professionals.

---

[4] As one dean put it: "It's not the role of the architect that is obsolete; it's the architects who are in it, and the way they define it as making sculpture. I want to expand it to include systematic follow-up and evaluation of the effects of design, testing whether assumptions that have been made are in fact valid."

References

Abercrombie, Margaret: *The Anatomy of Judgement,* Hutchinson Publishing Group, Ltd., London, 1960.

Abercrombie, Margaret: "Educating for Change," *University Quarterly,* vol. 20, pp. 7–16, 1966.

Abercrombie, Margaret: "Psychology and the Student," *AIA Journal,* September 1967.

Abercrombie, Margaret: "The Work of a University Education Research Unit," *University Quarterly,* vol. 22, pp. 182–196, 1968.

Abrahamson, M.: *The Professional in the Organization,* Rand-McNally & Company, Chicago, 1967.

"Architect–Community Connections," *IRTHE Bulletin,* University of Cincinnati Press, Cincinnati, undated.

Bailyn, Lotte, E. Schein, and H. Siler: "MIT Alumni Survey, Part 1: Where Are They Now?" unpublished report, Massachusetts Institute of Technology, 1971.

Barber, B.: "Some Problems in the Sociology of the Professions," *Daedalus,* vol. 92, pp. 669–688, 1963.

Becker, H. S., B. Geer, E. C. Hughes, and A. Strauss: *Boys in White: Student Culture in Medical School,* University of Chicago Press, Chicago, 1961.

Beckhard, R.: *Organization Development: Strategies and Models,* Addison-Wesley Publishing Company, Inc., Reading, Mass., 1969.

Bennis, W. G.: *Changing Organizations,* McGraw-Hill Book Company, New York, 1966.

Bennis, W. G.: *Organization Development: Its Nature, Origins, and Prospects,* Addison-Wesley Publishing Company, Inc., Reading, Mass., 1969.

Bennis, W. G., K. D. Benne, and R. Chin: *The Planning of Change,* 2d ed., Holt, Rinehart and Winston, Inc., New York, 1969.

Blau, P. M., and W. R. Scott: *Formal Organizations,* Chandler Publishing Company, San Francisco, 1962.

Boffey, P. M.: "Nader's Raiders on the FDA: Science and Scientists 'Misused,'" *Science,* vol. 168, pp. 349–352, 1970.

Boffey, P. M.: "Nader and the Scientists: A Call to Responsibility," *Science,* vol. 171, pp. 549–551, 1971.

Brown, G. W.: "Can Universities Fulfill the Challenge of Relevance?" *Technology Review,* vol. 72, pp. 25–31, 1970.

Christensen, P.: "A Proposal for the Development and Implementation of a Completely Modular Curriculum at the School of Education," unpublished proposal, University of Massachusetts, 1971.

"Concourse: A Proposal for a New Mode of Undergraduate Education for the First Two Years at MIT," unpublished proposal to the Committee on Educational Policy, Massachusetts Institute of Technology, 1971.

Considine, J.: "Outcomes of Self-Directed Education: A Study of the Alumni of the Undergraduate Systems Program of the MIT Sloan School of Management," *Alfred P. Sloan School Working Paper,* #435–69, Massachusettes Institute of Technology, 1969.

Crichton, M.: *Five Patients: The Hospital Explained,* Alfred A. Knopf, Inc., New York, 1970.

Davis, J. A.: *Undergraduate Career Decisions,* Aldine Publishing Company, Chicago, 1965.

Directory of MIT Undergraduate Research Opportunities, MIT Education Research Center, Cambridge, Mass., Spring 1971.

Drexler, A., and J. Wegener: "Innovative Teaching in Higher Education," *Human Relations Training News,* vol. 14, pp. 4–5, 1970.

Drucker, P.: "The Psychology of Managing Management: A Conversation with Mary Harrington Hall," *Psychology Today,* vol. 1, pp. 21–72, 1968.

Ehrlich, T., and T. Headrick: "The Changing Structure of Education at Stanford Law School," *Journal of Legal Education,* vol. 22, pp. 452–468, 1970.

Elbow, P.: "More Accurate Evaluation of Student Performance," *Journal of Higher Education,* vol. 40, pp. 219–230, 1969.

Evan, W. M.: "Due Process of Law in Military and Industrial Organizations," *Administrative Science Quarterly,* vol. 7, pp. 187–207, 1962.

"Fall Workshops," *IRTHE Bulletin,* University of Cincinnati Press, Cincinnati, undated.

Ferster, C.: "Individualized Instruction in a Large Introductory Psychology Course," unpublished manuscript, Georgetown University, 1968.

Field Study Centers Bulletin 1970–71, Union for Experimenting Colleges and Universities, Antioch College, Yellow Springs, Ohio.

Flaum, L.: "An Experiment with Independent Study," in L. Flaum (ed.), *Innovation and Innovative Program,* no. 22, University of South Carolina, Columbia, 1970.

Forrester, J. W.: "A New Avenue to Management," *Technology Review,* vol. 66, pp. 1–3, 1964.

Fox, Renee: "Training for Uncertainty," in M. Abrahamson (ed.), *The Professional in the Organization,* Rand-McNally & Company, Chicago, pp. 20–26, 1967.

Fry, R., and B. Lech: "An Organization Development Approach to Improving the Effectiveness of Neighborhood Health Care Teams: A Pilot Program," unpublished master's thesis, Sloan School of Management, Massachusetts Institute of Technology, 1971.

Geddes, R., and B. Spring: *A Study of Education for Environmental Design,* Princeton University, Princeton, N.J., 1967.

Gilb, Corinne L.: *Hidden Hierarchies,* Harper & Row, Publishers, Incorporated, New York, 1966.

Goode, W. J.: "Community Within a Community: The Professions," *American Sociological Review,* vol. 22, pp. 194–200, 1957.

Goodman, R.: "Liberated Zone: An Evolving Learning Space," *Harvard Educational Review,* vol. 39, pp. 86–97, 1969.

Green, B.: "A Self-Paced Course in Freshman Physics," *Occasional Papers,* MIT Education Research Center, Cambridge, Mass., 1969.

Gross, E.: "Change in Technological and Scientific Developments and Its Impact on the Occupational Structures," in R. Perrucci and J. Gerstl (eds.), *The Engineer and the Social System,* John Wiley & Sons, Inc., New York, 1969.

"Hampshire College: A Quest for Quality, A Balanced Budget," *Science,* vol. 170, pp. 954–958, 1970.

Hughes, E. C.: "Professions," *Daedalus,* vol. 92, pp. 655–668, 1963.

Keller, F. S.: "Good-Bye Teacher," *Journal of Applied Behavioral Analysis,* vol. 1, pp. 78–89, 1968.

Kolb, D.: "Individual Learning Styles and the Learning Process," *Alfred P. Sloan School Working Paper,* #535–71, Massachusetts Institute of Technology, 1971.

Kuhn, T.: *The Structure of Scientific Revolution,* revised ed., University of Chicago Press, Chicago, 1970.

"Law Students Work in Courts," *Stanford Observer,* p. 2, February 1971.

Lewin, K.: "Group Decision and Social Change," in T. Newcomb and E. Hartley (eds.), *Readings in Social Psychology,* Holt, Rinehart and Winston, Inc., New York, 1947.

Light, D. W.: *The Socialization and Training of Psychiatrists,* Ph.D. dissertation, Department of Sociology, Brandeis University, 1970.

"Living-Learning Cluster," *Time,* pp. 46–47, September 9, 1966.

Lomon, E.: "Seminar-Tutorial Program," unpublished notes for the Task Force on Educational Innovation, Massachusetts Institute of Technology, 1971.

Maclure, S.: "England's Open University," *Change,* vol. 3, pp. 62–68, 1971.

Marais, G.: "Management Training by Teletuition," *Management in the Future,* lecture delivered at the Third International Productivity Congress, Vienna, Hofburg, 1970.

Mayhew, L: *Changing Practices in Education for the Professions,* Southern Regional Education Board, Atlanta, in press.

Mayhew, L.: "Jottings," *Change,* vol. 2, pp. 81–83, 1970*a.*

Mayhew, L.: *Graduate and Professional Education, 1980,* McGraw-Hill Book Company, New York, 1970*b.*

McIntyre, J., and I. Rubin: "Report on Freshman Advisory Council Training," unpublished report, Massachusetts Institute of Technology, October 1969.

McGlothlin, W. J.: *The Professional Schools,* The Center for Applied Research in Education, Inc., New York, 1964.

Miles, M. B. (ed.): *Innovation in Education,* Bureau of Publications, Teachers College Press, Columbia University, New York, 1964.

Moore, W. E.: *The Professions: Roles and Rules,* Russell Sage Foundation, New York, 1970.

Morgan, Sandra: "The Unified Science Study Program," *The Science Teacher,* vol. 37, pp. 41–45, 1970.

Nader, R.: "The Engineer's Professional Role: Universities, Corporations, and Professional Societies," *The Journal of Engineering Education,* vol. 57, pp. 450–454, 1967.

Nader, R.: "Law Schools and Law Firms," *New Republic,* pp. 20–23, October 11, 1969.

"New Human Biology Program Attracts Three Hundred Students," *Stanford Observer,* p. 3, November 1970.

New York Times, The, pp. 1, 46, January 29, 1971.

Page, J. A.: "The Law Professor Behind ASH, SOUP, PUMP, and CRASH," *New York Times Magazine, The,* August 23, 1970.

Parlett, M., and J. King: "Concentrated Study, A Pedagogic Innovation Observed," *Research Into Higher Education Monographs,* no. 14, Society for Research Into Higher Education, London, 1971.

Parsons, T.: "Professions," *The International Encyclopedia of the Social Sciences,* The Macmillan Company, New York, 1968.

Parsons, T., and E. Shils (eds.): *Toward a General Theory of Action,* Harvard University Press, Cambridge, Mass., 1959.

Perrucci, R., and J. Gerstl: *Profession Without Community: Engineers in American Society,* Random House, Inc., New York, 1968.

Perrucci, R., and J. Gerstl (eds.): *The Engineer and the Social System,* John Wiley & Sons, Inc., New York, 1969.

Roe, Anne: "Community Resource Centers," *American Psychologist,* vol. 25, pp. 1033–1040, 1970.

Rothstein, W. G: "Engineers and the Functionalist Model of Professions," in R. Perrucci and J. Gerstl (eds.), *The Engineer and the Social System,* John Wiley & Sons, Inc., New York, 1969.

Sanford, N.: "Whatever Happened to Action Research?" *The Journal of Social Issues,* vol. 26, pp. 3–23, 1970.

Schein, E. H.: "Brainwashing," *The Yearbook of World Affairs,* Stevens and Sons, London, 1961.

Schein, E. H.: *Organizational Psychology,* Prentice-Hall, Inc., Englewood Cliffs, N.J., 1965.

Schein, E. H.: "The Problem of Moral Education for the Business Manager," *Industrial Management Review,* vol. 8, pp. 3–14, 1966.

Schein, E. H.: "A Proposed Seminar on Teaching," unpublished notes, Massachusetts Institute of Technology, 1967.

Schein, E. H.: "Organizational Socialization and the Profession of Management," *Industrial Management Review,* Third Douglas McGregor Memorial Lecture, vol. 9, pp. 1–15, 1968*a.*

Schein, E. H.: "Personal Change Through Interpersonal Relationships," in W. G. Bennis et al., *Interpersonal Dynamics,* revised ed., The Dorsey Press, Homewood, Ill., 1968*b.*

Schein, E. H.: *Process Consultation: Its Role in Organization Development,* Addison-Wesley Publishing Company, Inc., Reading, Mass., 1969.

Schein, E. H.: "The Reluctant Professor—Implications for University Management," *Sloan Management Review,* vol. 12, pp. 35–37, 1970*a.*

Schein, E. H.: "The Role Innovator and His Education," *Technology Review,* vol. 72, pp. 33–37, 1970*b.*

Schein, E. H., and W. G. Bennis: *Personal and Organizational Change through Group Methods: The Laboratory Approach,* John Wiley & Sons, Inc., New York, 1965.

Schiff, S. K.: "Training the Professional," *University of Chicago Magazine,* Fall 1970.

Scully, M.: "Experimental Programs Aim to Give Students Control of Their Education," *The Chronicle of Higher Education,* vol. 5, pp. 1–3, 1971.

Sommer, R.: *Personal Space, The Behavioral Basis of Design,* Prentice-Hall, Inc., Englewood Cliffs, N.J., 1969.

Speer, A.: *Inside the Third Reich,* The Macmillan Company, New York, 1970.

Sprague, C.: Unpublished and untitled address to the School of Architecture, University of Venice, November 1970.

Spurr, S. H.: *Academic Degree Structures: Innovative Approaches,* McGraw-Hill Book Company, New York, 1970.

Steele, F.: *Socio-Physical Organization Development,* Addison-Wesley Publishing Company, Inc., Reading, Mass., in press.

"The Study of Man," *Stanford Observer,* p. 3, February 1971.

The Union Graduate School, Antioch College, Yellow Springs, Ohio, March 1971.

Walsh, J.: "Stanford School of Medicine: Varieties of Medical Experience," *Science,* vol. 171, pp. 785–787, 1971.

Wilensky, H. L.: "The Professionalization of Everyone?" *American Journal of Sociology,* vol. 70, pp. 137–158, 1964.

Wisely, W. H.: Unpublished and untitled address to the American Society of Civil Engineers, November 11, 1970.

WPI News, Worcester Polytechnic Institute, Worcester, Mass., 1971.

Valley, G.: "A Qualitative Assessment of the MIT Experimental Studies Group," unpublished report, Massachusetts Institute of Technology, 1971.

Valley, G.: "Report to the Committee on Educational Policy Task Force on Educational Innovation," unpublished report, Massachusetts Institute of Technology, 1970.

Zacharias, J. R.: *Education Reform for the 70's,* MIT Education Research Center, Cambridge, Mass., 1970.

Zacharias, J. R.: "Professional Education of Scientists, Engineers, Physicians, and Teachers," unpublished reports, Massachusetts Institute of Technology, 1967.

Appendix: List of Persons Interviewed

Jane Abercrombie
Reader in Architectural Education
School of Environmental Studies
University College, London

Warren Bennis
President
University of Cincinnati

Robert Bishop
Dean, School of Humanities and
Social Studies
Massachusetts Institute of Tech-
nology

Gordon Brown
Professor and Former Dean
School of Engineering
Massachusetts Institute of Tech-
nology

Michael Cloutier
Dean, School of Management
Sherbrook University, Quebec

Frank Goudsmit
Berenschot Management Con-
sultants
Hengelo (O) The Netherlands

Paul Gray
Chancellor
Massachusetts Institute of Tech-
nology

Charles Handy
Director of Executive Development
Programs
London Business School

Sanford Hirschen
Professor of Architecture
University of California, Berkeley

Herbert Holloman
Consultant to the President and
the Provost, Massachusetts
Institute of Technology
Former President, University of
Oklahoma

Everett Hughes
Professor of Sociology
Boston College

Howard Johnson
Former President
Massachusetts Institute of Tech-
nology

Lawrence Kilham
Consultant on Educational Tech-
nology
Cambridge, Massachusetts

Sherman Kingsbury
Organization Consultant
Mill Valley, California

Gerald LaSalle, M.D.
Vice-Rector
Sherbrook University, Quebec

Daniel Levinson
Professor of Sociology
Yale Medical School

Donald Light
Professor of Sociology
Princeton University

Rosalynd Lindheim
Professor of Architecture
University of California, Berkeley

Donlyn Lyndon
Head, Department of Architecture
Massachusetts Institute of Technology

Lewis Mayhew
Professor of Education
Stanford University

Donald Michael
Director, Center for Utilization of Knowledge
University of Michigan

Roger Miller
Professor of Management
Sherbrook University, Quebec

Henry Millon
Professor of Architecture
Massachusetts Institute of Technology

John Myer
Professor of Architecture
Massachusetts Institute of Technology

Kenneth H. Myers
Dean, Division of Business
Southern Illinois University

John Peters, M.D.
Visiting Associate Professor
Sloan School of Management
Massachusetts Institute of Technology
Formerly, Associate Professor of Microbiology
Harvard University School of Public Health

William Porter
Dean, School of Architecture and Planning
Massachusetts Institute of Technology

William Pounds
Dean, Alfred P. Sloan School of Management
Massachusetts Institute of Technology

George Psathas
Director, Center for Applied Social Science
Boston University

Kimball Romney
Dean of Social Science
University of California, San Diego

Sherman Ross
Committee on Basic Research in Education
National Research Council

Frank Sander
Professor of Law
Harvard University

Irwin Sizer
Dean, Graduate School
Massachusetts Institute of Technology

Chester Sprague
Professor of Architecture
Massachusetts Institute of Technology

Fritz Steele
Consultant on Environmental Psychology and Behavioral Science
Boston, Massachusetts

Alan Stein
Staff Member, Human Relations Center
University of Cincinnati

William Terry
Attorney
Boston, Massachusetts

Robin Upton

Planning Consultant
Dober, Paddock & Upton
Cambridge, Massachusetts

George Valley

Professor and Director, Experi-
mental Study Group
Massachusetts Institute of Tech-
nology

John Vorenberg, M.D.

Boston, Massachusetts

Heather Weiss

Graduate Student, Harvard
Graduate School of Education
Consultant to the Waltham Forest
Polytechnic Institute
Walthamstow, England

Alan F. White

Director, Center for Cross-Cultural
Training and Research
University of Hawaii

Benjamin White

Professor of Psychology
University of San Francisco

Martha White

Consultant on Professional Career
Problems of Women
San Francisco, California

Jerome Wiesner

President
Massachusetts Institute of Tech-
nology

Carroll Wilson

Professor and Coordinator of
Undergraduate Policy Seminar
Program
Massachusetts Institute of Tech-
nology

Jerrold Zacharias

Director, Education Research
Center
Massachusetts Institute of Tech-
nology

Leonard Zegans, M.D.

Professor of Psychiatry
Yale Medical School

Index

*This book was set in Vladimir by University Graphics, Inc.
It was printed on acid-free, long-life paper and bound by The
Maple Press Company. The designers were Elliot Epstein and
Edward Butler. The editors were Nancy Tressel and Cheryl
Allen for McGraw-Hill Book Company and Verne A. Stadtman and
Terry Y. Allen for the Carnegie Commission on Higher Education.
Alice Cohen supervised the production.*